Revelations

Stephen Lowe

Methuen Drama

Published by Methuen 2003

1 3 5 7 9 10 8 6 4 2

Methuen Publishing Limited,
215 Vauxhall Bridge Road,
London SW1V 1EJ

Methuen Publishing Limited Reg. No. 3543167

A CIP catalogue record for this book is available from the British Library

ISBN 0 413 77419 8

Typeset by SX Composing DTP, Rayleigh, Essex
Printed and bound in Great Britain by
Cox & Wyman Ltd, Reading, Berkshire

hampstead theatre

HAMPSTEAD THEATRE PRESENTS THE WORLD PREMIERE OF

Revelations
by Stephen Lowe

Cast (in order of speaking)

Edward **Michael Elwyn**
Jeni **Julia Swift**
Emma **Rachel Sanders**
Tony **Gerald Kyd**
Shirley **Hetty Baynes**
Jimmy **Paul Slack**
Jack **Bertie Carvel**
Jill **Laura Rogers**

Director **Anthony Clark**
Designer **Rachel Blues**
Lighting **Jason Taylor**
Sound **Gregory Clarke**

Casting Director **Siobhan Bracke**
Assistant Director **Sam Leifer**
Wardrobe Supervisor **Laura Hunt**
Stage Manager **Suzanne Bourke**
Deputy Stage Manager **Sharon Cooper**
Assistant Stage Manager **Helena Lane-Smith**

Press Representative **Charlotte Eilenberg**
charlotte.eilenberg@dsl.pipex.com

Revelations was first performed at
Hampstead Theatre on 10 December 2003.

The text that follows was correct at the time
of going to print, but may have changed during rehearsal.

The Company

Stephen Lowe Writer

Stephen was born in Nottingham in 1947 and in 1966-70 took his degree in Theatre Arts/English at Birmingham University, going on to do postgraduate research. He did a variety of jobs whilst writing, before joining Alan Ayckbourn's Theatre in the Round as an actor, 1975-8. It was during this period that **Touched** won him the George Devine Award in 1977. He was Resident Playwright on the Theatre Degree course at Dartington College of Arts for four years (1978-82) and Resident Playwright at Riverside Studios in 1984. He has also run playwright workshops for the Arvon Foundation, the Royal Shakespeare Company and TV South West among others.

Theatre work includes: **Cards** (1971); **Stars** (1976); **Touched** (1977, Nottingham Playhouse directed by Richard Eyre and then on tour), the play won the George Devine Award and was revived in 1981 at the Royal Court directed by Bill Gaskill); **Shooting Fishing and Riding** (1977); **Sally Ann Hallelujah Band** (1977, Nottingham Playhouse); **The Ragged Trousered Philanthropist** (1978, Joint Stock then on tour, revived at Half Moon, Soho Rep New York); **Glasshouses** retitled **Moving Pictures** (1981, Royal Court Theatre directed by Bill Gaskill); **Strive** (1982); **Trial of Frankenstein** (1984); **Seachange** (1984, Riverside Studios directed by David Leveaux); **Keeping Body & Soul Together; Desire** (1986, Meeting Ground Theatre Company at Derby Playhouse and national tour); **Demon Lovers** (1987, Liverpool Playhouse and tour); translation of Ostrovsky's **The Storm** (1987, Royal Shakespeare Company at Barbican Pit); **Divine Gossip** (1988, Royal Shakespeare Company at Barbican Pit directed by Barry Kyle); adaptation of Schiller's **William Tell** (1989, Crucible Theatre, Sheffield); **Paradise** (1990, a musical for Nottingham Playhouse) and **The Alchemical Wedding** commission for Salisbury Playhouse which opened in 1998. Methuen publishes all of Stephen's stage plays.

Television and film work includes: **Fred Karno's Circus** (1978, BBC); **Cries from a Watchtower** (1980, BBC); **Shades** (1982, BBC); **Embrace** (1982, film commissioned by BFI); **Unstable Elements** (1984, 30' film for Newsreel Collective, fiction part of documentary for Channel 4 'Eleventh Hour'); **Kisses on the Bottom** (1985, BBC); **Ice Dance** (1989, BBC); **Flea Bites** (1992, BBC); **Tell Tale Hearts**, 3-part series (1992, BBC); **Stendhal's Le Rouge et Le Noir**, 3-part adaptation (transmitted Autumn 1993, BBC); **Coronation Street** (1994-1996); **Exit Lines - Dalziel and Pascoe** (1997, BBC) and **Greenstone,** 4 episodes (1998 Communicado, New Zealand).

Radio work includes **Touched** (1985, BBC Radio 4, adaptation of his stage play) and **The Daughter's Exhibition**.

Stephen is Founder and Co-Artistic Director of Meeting Ground Theatre for which he has written **Demon Lovers** (1989), **Desire** (1990) and **Paradise** (1992). He is also a council member of Arts Council England (ACE) and chair of ACE East Midlands.

Hetty Baynes Shirley

Hetty began her career as a ballet dancer at the Royal Ballet School and made her professional debut at 12 in Rudolf Nureyev's **The Nutcracker** at the Opera House, Covent Garden. She began her acting career at just 17 as an acting Assistant Stage Manager in repertory theatre.

Theatre includes: **The Country Wife** (Plymouth & tour); **The Heidi Chronicles, The Passing Out Parade, The Admirable Crichton** (Greenwich Theatre); **Women Laughing** - Best Actress nomination for the Manchester Evening News Awards (Manchester Royal Exchange); **The Philanthropist** (Wyndham Theatre); **Little Eyolf** - Best Actress nomination for the Fringe Awards (Birds Nest); **Hand Over Fist** (Watermill); **See How They Run, Theatre of Comedy** (Shaftesbury Theatre); **Buglar Boy** (Traverse Theatre, Edinburgh Festival); **Happy Event, The Reluctante Debutant, Hay Fever** (Windsor); **Le Bourgeois Gentilhomme** (Lyric, Belfast); **Chorus Girls** (Stratford East); **Suddenly Last Summer, Three Sisters** (Thorndike Theatre); **Inadmissible Evidence** (Royal Court); **Othello** (Ludlow Festival) and **The Merry Wives of Windsor, On the Rocks** (Mermaid Theatre).

Television includes **My Family, Cutting It, Cor Blimey, The Bill - A Time to Kill, Jonathan Creek, A Touch of Frost: Keys to the Car, Ken Russell's Treasure Island, The Vet, Alice in Russialand, The Darkening, Lady Chatterley, The Secret Life of Sir Arnold Bax, Minder VII, Old Flames, Christmas Present, London's Burning, Harry's Kingdom, Bergerac, The Piglet Files, Drummonds, Tropical Moon Over Dorking, Wynne & Penkovsky, Chance in a Million, Dickens of London, Running Scared, Charters & Caldicott, Marjorie and Men, Crime Writers, Just William, Good Companions, Winter Sunlight, Mystery of the Seven Dials, Dombey and Sons, Sense & Sensibility, Nicholas Nickleby, Benefit of the Doubt, The Last Song, Hunchback of Notre Dame, Renoir My Father** and Stephen Lowe's play for the BBC, **Kisses on the Bottom**, about the seaside postcard characters in which she played Vera, the 'buxom blonde'.

Her numerous radio performances include **Rumpole and the Vanishing Juror, Tim Merryman's Days of Clover**, Suzy in the radio soap **Citizens** and Marilyn Monroe in **Anyone Can See I Love You** - nominated for Best Actress at the Sony and PrixItalia Awards.

Film includes **Coping with Cupid, The Insatiable Mrs Kirsch** which she co wrote with Ken Russell, **Mindbender, The Life of Uri Geller** and Herbert Ross's **Nijinsky**.

Bertie Carvel Jack

Bertie trained at RADA after earning a first class degree in English from the University of Sussex.

Revelations is his professional theatre debut.

Since graduating this summer, his credits include **Hawking** for BBC Television and **The Pallisers** for BBC Radio. He has also appeared in two short films, **Artificial Light** and **Suits and Swipes,** and was runner-up in this year's Carleton Hobbs competition.

Michael Elwyn Edward

Recent theatre includes: **Darwin in Malibu** (Birmingham Repertory Theatre); **Broken Glass** (West Yorkshire Playhouse); **A Midsummer Night's Dream, Troilus and Cressida, All's Well That Ends Well** (Open Air Theatre, Regent's Park); **Strangers on a Train, Vertigo, Otherwise Engaged** (Guildford and UK tours); **Jumpers** (Norwich Playhouse); **Emma** (Cambridge Theatre Co); **The Seagull, We, the Undersigned, The Secret Life, The Way to Keep Him, A Penny for a Song,** (Orange Tree, Richmond); **Safe In Our Hands** (Belgrade, Coventry); **Love on the Plastic** (Half Moon Theatre) and **Nothing Sacred** (Theatre Clwyd).

Recent television includes **Byron, Daniel Deronda, Bad Girls, Bertie and Elizabeth, Micawber, North Square, Plain Jane, Silent Witness, Big Bad World, Border Café, The Knock, Dirty Work, Stagestruck, The Bill, Heartbeat, The Blind Date, Heat of the Sun, Life and Crimes of William Palmer,**

Soldier Soldier, This Life, No Bananas, A Pleasant Terror, The Governor, Fireworks, Between the Lines, Ruth Rendell Mysteries, Framed, After Henry, Inspector Alleyn, The Orchid House, Selling Hitler, Kinsey, Sam Saturday, Streets Apart and **A Piece of Cake.**

Films include **A Touch of Class, The French Lieutenant's Woman, Half Moon Street, The Private Life of Sherlock Holmes, Decline and Fall, Crimestrike, Jinnah** and **Dot the i.**

Michael is a regular reader for BBC's **Poetry Please, With Great Pleasure** and **Great Lives.**

Gerald Kyd Tony

Theatre includes: **Edward II, Richard II** (Globe Theatre); **Deathtrap** (No. 1 tour / PW Prod.); **The Pit and the Pendulum** (Windsor / Bromley); **Love's Labours Lost** (English Touring Theatre); **Ramayana** (Birmingham Repertory Theatre); **The Local Stigmatic** (Lyric Studio, Hammersmith); **Prophet in Exile** (Chelsea Centre) and **Cyrano de Bergerac** (Royal Shakespeare Company, Stratford / tour / West End).

Television includes **Grease Monkeys, Life & Times of William Shakespeare, Casualty** (series 13 & 14), **The Professionals** and **Underworld.**

Film includes **Tomb Raider II** and **Principles of Lust.**

Laura Rogers Jill

Laura trained at RADA.

Theatre includes: **Taming of the Shrew, Richard III** (Globe Theatre); **Hayfever** (Oxford Stage Company); **Blackwater Angel** (Abbey Theatre); **Present Laughter** (Battersea Arts Centre) and **Arcadia** (Lyric Hammersmith).

Television includes: **Rockface, Running Scared, Relic Hunter, Tales of Pleasure Beach** and **The Sins.**

Film includes: **The Right Hand Man** and **Moving Still.**

Rachel Sanders Emma

Rachel trained at the Welsh College of Music and Drama.

Recent theatre includes: **The Bacchai** (National Theatre); **Othello** (National Theatre at the William Poel Festival); **Richard III, Taming of the Shrew** (Globe Theatre); A **Servant to Two Masters, Richard III, Faust, La Nuit de Valgones, Romeo and Juliet, The Cherry Orchard** (Royal Shakespeare Company) and **The Four Seasons, The Journey of Mary Kelly, A Christmas Carol** (CTC).

Other theatre includes: **Mother Courage, The Tempest** (Shared Experience); **Silence**

(Birmingham Repertory Theatre); **The Farmer's Bride** (Wild Iris Theatre) and **Elvis Is Alive...** (Edinburgh Festival).

Television and film includes **Starhunter 2300, The Bill, Coronation Street, Picking Up the Pieces, The Wyvern Mystery, Double Exposure, Thicker Than Water** and **The Auctioneer.**

Paul Slack Jimmy

Theatre includes: **The Master Builder, The Seagull** (English Touring Theatre); **Neville's Island, Time and the Conways** (Bristol Old Vic); **Privates on Parade** (Greenwich Theatre and on tour); **The Comedy of Errors, Big Night Out, Paradise, King Lear** (Nottingham Playhouse); **Breaking the Code** (Haymarket Theatre and on tour); **The Pope & the Witch** (Comedy Theatre); **Comedians** (Lyric, Hammersmith); **Getting Attention** (Royal Court); **A Midsummer Night's Dream, The Beaux Stratagem** (Royal Shakespeare Company); **The Gulf Between Us, Second from Last in the Sack Race, Pratt of the Argus, In All Innocence,** (West Yorkshire Playhouse); **American Buffalo, Mystery Plays, Sea Monkeys** (Sheffield Crucible); **The Rover, The Banished Cavalier** (Salisbury Playhouse); **Night Must Fall** (Theatre Clwyd); **The Playboy of the Western World** (Oldham

Coliseum) and **Phoenix Rising – The Young D. H. Lawrence** (Nottingham Playhouse, West Yorkshire Playhouse and on tour).

Television includes **Shipman, As Time Goes By, Heartbeat, Always and Everyone, Peak Practice, The Bill, Casualty, A Touch of Frost, The Governor, Trial by Jury, Hetty Wainthrop Investigates, Wing and a Prayer, Between the Lines, Divorce's Deadliest Weapon, Fair Game, 99-1, Running Late** and **The Monocled Mutineer.**

Film includes **Love Actually, Heartlands, Bright Young Things** and **Holding On.**

Julia Swift Jeni

London theatre includes: **Orpheus Descending** (Donmar Warehouse); **Suddenly Last Summer** (Comedy Theatre); **Broken Glass** (National Theatre); **In the Summertime** (Lyric Hammersmith); **Time and the Conways** (Old Vic); **Chekhov's Women** (Lyric); **The Seagull** (Gielgud); **A Midsummer Night's Dream** (Open Air Theatre, Regents Park); **The Relapse** (Old Vic); **Royal Borough, Ambulance** (Royal Court Theatre Upstairs); **German Connection** (Young Vic Studio) and **Exceptions** (New End Theatre). For the Royal Shakespeare Company **Two Gentlemen of Verona, All's Well that Ends Well** and **Electra**.

Regional theatre includes: **Arms and the Man, The Merchant, The Father, The**

Tempest, Arturo Ui, Lady Windermere's Fan and **The Three Sisters.**

Theatre on Broadway, **The Merchant of Venice.**

Television includes: **The Caucasian Chalk Circle, Ladies in Charge, Shalom, Joan Collins, Nativity Blues** and **Salad Days.** Guest appearances include **Holby City, Midsomer Murders, London Bridge, The Bill** and **The Royal.**

Film includes: **The Sailor's Return, Broken Glass** and many radio performances

Anthony Clark Director

Anthony started his career as Assistant Director at the Orange Tree Theatre where he directed everything from a schools tour of **Macbeth** to Martin Crimp's first play, **Living Remains.**

He spent six years as Artistic Director of Contact Theatre in Manchester, where his favourite productions include **A Midsummer Night's Dream, The Duchess of Malfi, Blood Wedding** (Manchester Evening News Best Production Award), **Mother Courage and Her Children, Oedipus Rex, To Kill A Mockingbird** (Manchester Evening News Best Production Award), **The Power of Darkness,** and new plays **Two Wheeled Tricycle, Face Value, Green, Homeland,** and **McAlpine's Fusiliers,** before joining Birmingham Repertory Theatre as Associate Artistic Director. His productions there include **Macbeth, Julius Caesar, Atheist's Tragedy** (TMA Best Director Award), **The Seagull, Of Mice and Men, Threepenny Opera, Saturday Sunday Monday, The Grapes of Wrath, The Playboy of The Western World, Pygmalion, Gentlemen Prefer Blondes** (the play), **St Joan, The Entertainer** and the premiere of David Lodge's **Home Truths.**

In 1997 he was responsible for launching and programming The Door (formerly The Rep Studio), dedicated exclusively to promoting new plays. The new plays he directed for The Door include **Playing by The Rules** by Rod Dungate, **Nervous Women** by Sara Woods, **Rough** by Kate Dean, **Syme** by Michael Bourdages, **True Brit** by Ken Blakeson, **Confidence** by Judy Upton, **Down Red Lane** by Kate Dean, **Paddy Irishman** by Declan Croghan, **All That Trouble** by Paul Lucas, **Silence** by Moira Buffini, **My Best Friend** by Tamsin Oglesby, **Slight Witch** by Paul Lucas, and **Belonging** by Kaite O'Reilly.

He has freelanced extensively including **Dr Faustus** (The Young Vic), **The Red Balloon** (Bristol Old Vic / National Theatre, TMA Best Show for Young People Award), **The Snowman** (Leicester Haymarket), **Mother Courage and Her Children** (National Theatre), **The Day After Tomorrow** (National Theatre), **The Wood Demon** (The Playhouse) **Loveplay** by Moira Buffini (Royal Shakespeare Company) and **Edward III** (Royal Shakespeare Company).

This is Anthony's first season as Artistic Director of Hampstead Theatre, for which he also directed **The Maths Tutor** by Clare McIntyre.

Rachel Blues Designer

Rachel's designs for director Anthony Clark include: **Loveplay** (Royal Shakespeare Company / Pit); **Krindlekrax** (Birmingham Repertory Theatre / Nottingham Playhouse) and **Silence, Belonging, Winnie the Witch** (Birmingham Repertory Theatre).

Her other credits include: **The Deep Blue Sea** (Theatre Royal Bath / Richmond Theatre / No 1 tour); **A Doll's House** and **Mongoose** (Southwark Playhouse); **Dinner, Free, Life After Life** (National Theatre Loft); **The Cherry Orchard** (Oxford Stage Company / Riverside Studio); **Top Girls** (OSC, Aldwych / tour); **Ham!** (New Vic Theatre Stoke); **The Dove** (Croydon Warehouse); **Bouncers** (Bolton Octagon) and **Intimate Death** (Gate Theatre).

Rachel was resident designer at the Coliseum Theatre for two seasons where she designed nine productions and for the Swan Theatre Worcester where she designed **Private Lives** and **Charley's Aunt.**

She has also designed **Meteorite** which is currently running at Hampstead Theatre during the daytime.

Jason Taylor Lighting

Current and recent work includes: **Tom's Midnight Garden** (Birmingham Repertory Theatre / national tour); **Excuses** (ATC / Soho Theatre); **Airsick** (Bush Theatre / Drum Theatre Plymouth); **Madness of George III, Little Shop of Horrors** (West Yorkshire Playhouse); **US and Them, The Dead Eye Boy** (Hampstead Theatre); **Protection, Wrong Place** (Soho Theatre); **Hobson's Choice, Yerma** (Manchester Royal Exchange); **Abigail's Party** (New Ambassadors Theatre / Whitehall Theatre / national tour); **Pretending to be Me** (Comedy Theatre); **My Night with Reg / Dealers Choice** (Birmingham Repertory Theatre); **The Clearing** (Shared Experience); **Single Spies** (national tour); **Sitting Pretty** (national tour); **Pirates of Penzance** (national tour); **Office** (Edinburgh International Festival); **Hedda Gabler, Snake in Fridge** (Manchester Royal Exchange); **Iolanthe, The Mikado, Yeoman of the Guard** (Savoy Theatre) and last year's Labour Party Conference.

Jason has lit over 200 other productions including: 14 seasons at the Open Air Theatre; **Kindertransport** (Vaudeville Theatre); **Rosencrantz and Guildenstern** (Piccadilly Theatre); **And Then There Were None** (Duke of York's Theatre) and **Great Balls of Fire** (Cambridge Theatre). Other London work includes productions at the Bush Theatre, Hampstead Theatre, Bridewell Theatre and numerous productions for Soho Theatre. Jason has also designed at most major regional theatres including Nottingham, Sheffield, Plymouth, West Yorkshire Playhouse, Birmingham, Edinburgh, Scarborough, Southampton, Clwyd and Liverpool. Jason was also lighting consultant for the new Soho Theatre, London and the Open Air Theatre, Regents Park.

Gregory Clarke Sound

Gregory's sound design credits include: **Abigail's Party** (The New Ambassadors Theatre / Whitehall Theatre); **Mum's the Word** (Albery Theatre); **Lady Windermere's Fan, The Royal Family** (Theatre Royal, Haymarket); **Song Of Singapore** (Mayfair Theatre, London) and **No Man's Land** (National Theatre).

For the Royal Shakespeare Company: **Merry Wives of Windsor** (The Old Vic / Stratford / USA Tour); **Coriolanus** (The Old Vic / Stratford); and **Tantalus** (Stratford / UK Tour).

Other theatre includes: **The Two Gentlemen of Verona, Loves Labour's Lost** (Open Air Theatre, Regent's Park); **Abigail's Party, The Dead Eye Boy, Snake, Gone To LA, Terracotta, Local Boy, Buried Alive, Tender** (Hampstead Theatre); **Semi-Detached, Pal Joey, Heartbreak House, A Small Family Business** (Chichester Festival Theatre); **The Cherry Orchard, Demons and Dybbuks, The Black Dahlia** (Method & Madness); **Nathan The Wise, Song Of Singapore, Nymph Errant** (Minerva Theatre, Chichester); **Design for Living, Betrayal, Fight For Barbara, As You Like It** (The Peter Hall Company Season at the Theatre Royal Bath); **Office Suite, Present Laughter** (Theatre Royal Bath); the new musical **Baiju Bawra** (Theatre Royal, Stratford East); **Dick Whittington** (Stratford East at Greenwich); **Krindlekrax** (Birmingham Repertory Theatre); **The Hackney Office** (Druid Theatre, Galway), **Beyond A Joke** (Yvonne Arnaud Theatre, co-design with John Leonard) and **Dumped, A Midsummer Night's Dream** (National Youth Theatre).

hampstead theatre

Hampstead Theatre moved into its new RIBA award winning building in February 2003 after over 40 years in a portacabin that was only expected to last for 10 years.

Our new theatre, designed by Bennetts Associates, is home to a fully adaptable elliptical auditorium seating up to 325, and The Space – a studio space for our expanding work with local schools and the local community.

Continuing Hampstead Theatre's policy of producing new plays by both established and emerging writers, the opening season included plays by Tim Firth, Debbie Tucker Green, Stephen Adly Guirgis, Tanika Gupta and Tamsin Oglesby.

'A delight inside: warm, dramatic, visually appealing and imaginatively planned. A splendid home for new writing' THE DAILY TELEGRAPH

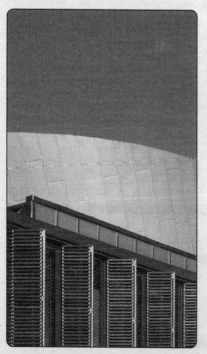

Anthony Clark's first season as Artistic Director includes plays from established writers Clare McIntyre, Stephen Lowe and Hanif Kureishi; the second play from the multi-award winning playwright Gregory Burke; an exceptional first play from a young Canadian poet living in London, Drew Pautz; and an original play by Barbara Norden for

7 – 11 year olds and their families – the start of a plan to see more plays for children presented at Hampstead Theatre.

All the plays in the season share a passion on the part of the writers to explore the contemporary world. The writing is inquisitive, imaginative and revealing – trying to make sense of experiences we share while introducing us to new worlds. Qualities that are the hallmark of the commissioning policy of Hampstead Theatre.

Education & Participation Programme

Since its inception in 1998, we have had over 58,000 attendances from aspiring writers and actors aged 5 to 85. Our new home houses a large, dedicated education studio, The Space, which can be transformed from a workshop into a fully equipped performance studio with ease and speed. Local residents and schools are encouraged to make use of the Theatre's expertise and facilities through a number of different projects.

To find out more visit our website, talk to us on 020 7449 4165 or email education@hampsteadtheatre.com

Start Nights

A great chance to see the talent of the future flexing its creative muscle.

Start Nights are also an opportunity to present twenty minutes of new material to an audience and gauge their feedback.

Anyone over the age of 16 living, working or studying in London can participate. Ask at the box office for entry details or check our website.

Start Nights are sponsored by Habitat with support from Arts & Business New Partners.

Priority Supporters

With advance information and priority booking you can be the first to discover fresh and dynamic playwrights, and make the most of a whole range of discounts for just £12 a year. For more details call us on 020 7722 9301 or email info@hampsteadtheatre.com

Cafébar

Open 9.00am to 11.00pm Monday to Saturday, the cafébar offers a generous selection of sandwiches, baguettes, warm paninis, pastas and salads.

You can also order a pre-show supper or an interval snack ahead of time by calling us on 020 7722 9301. Check our website for more information.

Our new building is a stunning venue for celebrations or conferences. For further details email conferencing@hampsteadtheatre.com or talk to us on 020 7034 4914.

Supporting Hampstead Theatre

Luminaries

By becoming one of Hampstead Theatre's Luminaries, you will be giving vital support to all aspects of our work, and become more involved with the theatre. There are three levels of support and a variety of benefits offered including priority booking, a dedicated booking line, crediting in playtexts and programmes and invitations to exclusive events. Membership starts at £250 per year.

Our current Luminaries are:

Level 1
Anonymous
Michael & Leslie Bennett
Deborah Buzan
Denis & Ronda Cassidy
Richard Curtis
Frankie de Freitas
Robyn Durie
George Fokschaner
Richard Gladstone
Elaine & Peter Hallgarten
Lew Hodges
Patricia & Jerome Karet
Richard & Ariella Lister
Tom & Karen Mautner
Judith Mishon & Philip Mishon OBE
Trevor Phillips
Tamara & Michael Rabin
Barry Serjent
Dr Michael Spiro
Marmont Management Ltd.
Hugh Whitemore & Rohan McCulloch
Dr Adrian Whiteson & Mrs Myrna Whiteson
Peter Williams
Debbie & Derek Zissman

Level 2
Dorothy & John Brook
Professor & Mrs C J Dickinson
Matthew & Alison Green
The Mackintosh Foundation
Midge & Simon Palley
Michael & Olivia Prior
Anthony Rosner
Judy Williams

Level 3
Richard Peskin

Corporate Partners

Hampstead Theatre is proud to launch its Corporate Partners scheme. This offers a flexible package of benefits with which you can entertain your clients, promote your business objectives and take advantage of everything that the new theatre has to offer. Corporate Partners membership is available from £5,000 + VAT.

Our current Corporate Partners are:

Bennetts Associates Architects

habitat®

CHAMPAGNE
TAITTINGER
Reims

SOLOMON TAYLOR & SHAW SOLICITORS

We offer a range of other sponsorship opportunities, from performance sponsorship, project support, production sponsorship, gala event sponsorship, education support or even title sponsorship for the entire season. Benefits can be tailored to your needs – please talk to us for more information.

To find out more about Luminaries, Corporate Partners or other ways to support us, please contact Sarah Coop in our Development Department on 020 7449 4160 or email development@hampsteadtheatre.com.

Support Us

If there is a particular area of our work that you would like to support, please talk to us. We have numerous projects available covering all aspects of our work from education to play development.

As a registered charity, Hampstead Theatre can accept donations from charitable trusts and foundations, gifts of stocks and shares, donations via CAF America or in a tax-efficient manner under the Gift Aid scheme. Making the declaration is simple – contact the Development Team for more information.

Legacies
Why not consider leaving a legacy to the theatre? This gives us lasting support well into the future. You can leave a gift to support a new commission, to fund education work or leave it open for us to use it in the area of most need.

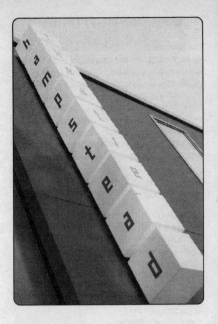

Hampstead Theatre's Supporters
2003/04

Abbey National Charitable Foundation – Supporting Sign Interpreted Performances
ADAPT Trust – Barry Foster Memorial Award for Excellence in Access, 2003
Arts & Business New Partners
Auerbach Trust Charity
Bridge House Estates Trust Fund
Champagne Taittanger
Deutsche Ag Bank
Lloyds TSB Foundation for England and Wales
Reed Elsevier

Naming Seats
We have released the remaining seats in the auditorium of the new theatre to be named. The seats in the initial batch were all named before the new theatre opened in February 2003. Why not name a seat after yourself, your children, in memory of a loved one or to promote your business? Seats are available from £1,500 and payments can be spread over 3 years.

For more information on any of these or if you would like to support the theatre in another way, please contact Sarah Coop in the Development Department on 020 7449 4160 or email development@hampsteadtheatre.com.

Revelations

New Nation

Introduction

Lord Illingworth   The Book of Life begins with a man and a woman in a garden.
Mrs Allonby   It ends with Revelations.

A Woman of No Importance by Oscar Wilde

I started with one particular woman in a garden – the garden of England. I was researching for a film idea based on the Godiva legend and the first site conjured up on the Internet by her magic name was the Godiva Swingers – based in California – no surprises there! Although her ladyship might have been a little unsure about their particular version of bare-back riding they were (as befits Californians) utopian in their liberal ideals and emphatically laid down their humanistic 'free-love' code. At the time it was just a mere curiosity, conjuring up an image of fading hippies romping in the sunset of the Big Sur.

The next story to interest me was set in the English version of the Big Sur – Bridlington, a seaside town of almost unimpeachable boredom. The tabloids had got hold of a juicy tale. A woman, unhappy with her divorce settlement, was suing her husband (a local butcher) for mental cruelty in that he had 'persuaded' her into joining the swingers scene, and 'corrupted' her in the process. Newspapers waved cheque books for full confessions, other participants were named (and shamed), the husband was portrayed as a vile seducer/pimp and pervert, the wife as the innocent victim – shades of *Justine* and *The Story of O*. Children were alerted to their parents' sexual proclivities, ordinary people were 'outed', jobs were lost, relationships shattered. If the west-coast swingers were openly stuck in some Tantric position, here it was clear that we were still trapped in the world of the witch hunt, with all its traditional prurience, its intense and obsessive searching for marks of the devil – the moles, the love-bites – its dark fascination with the sabbat and the kissing of the satanic master's arse, and its need of course finally to punish. The punishment is the trial, the public spectacle. For the rest of us it was a joke, a snigger, a shiver. And the only cost was the pennies for the paper. For the reader at any rate.

I was outraged. Media intrusion into private activities between consenting adults seems to me something we should be outraged by, and I began to research and map out a potential television serial set around the repercussions of a swingers' weekend that led towards a tragic conclusion. The view of the TV companies was basically that no one would sympathise with characters who went beyond the normally defined heterosexual frontiers. (Unless of course they were about Byron or people who lived in Bloomsbury in the twenties). Or that I wasn't 'judging' them enough – that I was unprepared to say that the route they had taken was wrong, that they'd stepped into the darkness and inevitably (and justly) got burned. Frankly, it didn't seem a God-given certainty that their transgression had to lead automatically to hellfire. So I decided to spare them the tragedy and search for a kind of comedy *against the odds*.

And as you might suspect, it produced an *odd comedy*. Quite how odd took me by surprise. Most 'sex' comedies are about people attempting to have illicit relationships whilst desperately hiding the fact from their regular partners. And the gag is how difficult it is for them to attain that as they dart in and out of cupboards, wardrobes, hotel doors.

The force of attempted infidelity and feverish frustration? *Revelations* inverts this. Here the couples are attempting a new kind of honesty in terms of their own relationship whilst hiding their identity from the rest of the world. They set out, at least initially, together into an uncertain world of desire. Do they fare any better? Or any worse? Is such honesty itself possible?

The face of attempted fidelity and feverish fulfilment? Shirley, group leader for this beginners' swinging evening, remarks: 'Life. You go through one door and you're in one world, walk through another and you're in a completely different one t'other.'

What's the 't'other' they've walked into? What is the world of swinging? Is it a new phenomenon, or does it have ancient roots? Well, of course there have always been orgies. The word itself originally referred to the Dionysian

bacchanals. And they've reoccurred throughout history –
the Mayday revels, Venetian masked balls, the underground
parties of the HellFire Club. And nowadays, apparently, any
18–30 group holiday in Ibiza! But *swinging* adds a new twist
to the old game. Whereas in the past people often went
masked and alone into the shadows of the night, swinging
centres on the *sanctity* of the heterosexual partnership – the
couple who have decided to cross the line of desire *together*.

And since its arrival in the 'swinging sixties' the nature of
its transgression has also changed. Once it was 'wife-
swapping' – Postman's Knock for adults. Throw your keys
onto the coffee table and go off with a different partner for
the same kind of one-on-one (male–female) sexual
encounter and back home to bed with hubby or wife and a
cup of hot chocolate. And probably the same unspoken and
disturbing questions – *was he/she better than me*? A risky
mirroring of a probably already fragile relationship. Perhaps
for understandable reasons the keys have been largely
abandoned, to be replaced by a more orgiastic encounter –
a kind of secret, underground theatre where 'performer' and
'audience' are radically re-aligned, where exhibitionism and
voyeurism combine for mutual satisfaction. And sets,
costumes and acting are essential elements of a dangerous
game. Here honesty is the key word, whilst endless lies are
necessary to avoid exposure, and at the same time another
kind of exposure is to be celebrated. A world of paradox, of
illusion, of fantasies, and of reality. Fertile ground for at
least the imagination of this one writer to explore.

The most common word in the swinger's lexicon is the
word 'play'. Swinging is intended to be 'fun' – that
quintessentially English word which summons up images of
fairgrounds and seaside rides – the escape from suffocating
mundanity. Play. It may turn out to have darker elements to
it but that is its aspiration.

I feel rather the same about my own play. I hope you
enjoy it.

Stephen Lowe
November 2003

Revelations

'The subject of art should be the three topics
unsuitable for discussion at an English tea
party – politics, religion and sex.'
                    – James Joyce (Stephen Hero)

'The difficulty is telling them apart.'
                              (Stephen Lowe)

'The first and wisest of them all professed to
know this only, that he nothing knew . . .'
                    Milton, Paradise Regained, IV.293

Characters

Edward, *late forties*
Jeni, *mid-forties*
Emma, *early thirties*
Tony
Shirley, *late thirties*
Jimmy, *late thirties*
Jack
Jill

Time: the present.
Place: a conservatory in the Lake District.

Act One

The Conservatory.

Dark. Chopin's piano nocturne Opus 32, number 2 softly playing.

A brilliantly back-lighted stained-glass triptych of a Pre-Raphaelite
ADAM *and* **EVE** *on either side of an apple tree miraculously both in*
full blossom and burdened with its crimsoned fruit. Entwined around
the trunk – the snake. It is not immediately apparent that the **ADAM**
and **EVE** *panels are both doors to the house beyond.* **Edward** *(late*
forties, in jeans and Tate T-shirt) clumsily uses a remote to control the
back-lighting to focus on varying aspects of the triptych.

Edward *(nervous)*   'Come into the garden, Maud/The
black bat, night, has flown/Come into the garden, Maud/I
am here at the gate, alone.' Tennyson. Well, you knew that,
didn't you? I mean everybody, I wasn't implying in any way
that you didn't . . . Actually, strangely in respect to that . . .
there's actually a very fine charcoal sketch by Dante Gabriel
Rossetti of Tennyson actually reading that very poem at the
Barrett Brownings. Must have been a very stimulating
evening, I would have loved to have . . . Fly on the wall,
buzz, the curious thing is no one present seemed to be
aware of Rossetti actually doing it. He'd hid himself away in
the shadows . . . Complete secret. Like this place, in effect.
Not that there's any secret Rossetti and his Pre-Raphaelite
brethren were in love with the Lake District, indeed some of
Burne-Jones's finest stained-glass windows can be seen just
down the mountainside in Brampton. St Martin's Church.
If the snow ever stops or we tire of . . . But what is a secret,
although shortly to be exposed in my own . . . No . . . We
now know the Brotherhood all stayed here together at one
time and used this remarkable conservatory as a setting for
their works. The folly's owner was Sir Henry Ecclestone, a
Mancunian top hat with taste, some of it admittedly verging
on the erotic, if not indeed the downright pornographic.
And we should thank him for that, if only for this one
extraordinary hidden gem. The Garden. Here for once the

artist felt sufficiently free from the restraints of the choking
Victorian morality to lift the clouds from the lower valleys
literally, to halt the sigh of the zephyr from swirling lost
shreds of cloth across the loins, to leave the fig leaves
fluttering high upon the bough. And look at the tree of
knowledge – the apple tree, and what an extraordinary tree,
both in blossom and fruit at one and the same time. A
wondrous ripe impossibility in its sheer burgeoning sexual
potential and its immediate promise of fulfilment. Truly a
garden of paradise. Eve here is unquestionably the former
prostitute Fanny Cornforth, Adam her lover Rossetti,
whether a self-portrait or sketched by some other brother
hidden in the shadows as they reclaimed the garden, in a
wondrous dance of erotic folly through the erratic folly itself,
in a delirium of release, of artists, muses, models, whores,
angels, innocence entwined with experience, a madrigal of
madness, pulsating polka, questioning, searching, fighting to
break through the lace-fringed Victorian hypocrisy, not just
in the art itself but in life, for art and life were as one, such
divisions were a false tyranny of duality. Everything had to
be transgressed, transgression itself was the core of their
young and burning creed. Some fell by the wayside later,
some were burnt, some recanted, some held up a different
light of the world. All in fear had to veil the real truth.
(*Pause.*) It seemed to me . . . for us . . . we too, trapped, but
yearning. Ready to transgress, to break through. To return.
It seemed to me that, having seen only imperfect images of
each other on the internet, this was the perfect setting for
our first meeting, here in the secret garden. What the hell
am I doing here?

A shadow and EVE*'s door opens propelling him down into the
conservatory. His wife,* **Jeni**, *petite, mid-forties. She carries a tray of
vol-au-vents.*

Jeni   Lights, Edward, lights.

Edward   Sorry, sorry.

*As he tries to rebalance the lighting he reveals the ornate cast-iron hot-
house of potted plants, palms, ivy and nineteenth-century classical*

statuettes. A raised dais with fountain that bubbles into life. The descent of a few steps to the main area arranged with expensive loungers and cushions. The carefully placed lighting offers a whole wealth of different atmospheres. The side windows running with condensation. Outside night, ice and snow. (NB **Edward** *will nervously play with the lighting throughout the evening, constantly looking for the 'right' tone.)*

Jeni (*blinded by a strong spot*)   I'm blinded.

Edward   Difficult to control this damned thing.

Jeni (*looking down at the cushions*)   Mind you, perhaps it's better I can't see. Oh, God.

She pours herself a drink.

Edward   You don't think you've had enough?

Jeni   'The road of excess leads to the palace of wisdom.' Your title page quote. 'Transgression and the Pre-Raphaelites.' The hidden truth. I love it, Edward, you know that . . . God, I typed the manuscript . . . I just hadn't . . . I presumed it was a pure piece of academic research. I hadn't grasped it was a do-it-yourself manual. Stupid of me.

Edward   Jeni, we've discussed this a thousand times.

Jeni   Grapes.

Edward   What?

Jeni   Forgot the grapes. How can you have an orgy without grapes? Cecil B. De Mille wouldn't have dreamt of it and he's the expert. Grapes, Oysters, togas. (*Pause.*) And sandals. God, the thought of Englishmen in just their sandals and socks. That won't happen . . . Will it? The thought . . . Don't let me forget the sausage rolls. The Aga. Oh, God, Edward, I can just about cope with one of your faculty parties, but not with an orgy.

Edward   You think they weren't?

Jeni   I don't recall writing it on the invites.

Edward   Deceit and sexual betrayal, that's all they ever were.

Jeni   And is this in some way different?

Edward   Utterly.

Jeni   Utterly. How?

Edward   We are here together, sharing.

Jeni   Sharing what?

Edward (*pauses*)   Our uncertainties.

Jeni   True. I've never been more uncertain in my life. But . . . I realise this is the eleventh hour but I just wonder . . . couldn't we start building our new life out of our certainty instead?

Edward   And what is that?

Jeni   Our love?

Silence.

Edward   Sooner or later we have to face our fears.

Jeni   Is that absolutely essential? I mean, you know I'm terrified of spiders, I have this instant panic whenever I see a bunch of bananas that if I pull one off there'll be a giant furry thing underneath. Of course, that's probably Freudian, isn't it, but to be honest, I don't mind living without bananas. Too much starch anyway. (*Shaking.*) This is ridiculous. I can't go through with it. I'll end up hallucinating tarantulas and singing the banana boat song with my knickers over my head.

Edward   It shouldn't be like this, Jeni . . . I mean we've tried . . . (*Sighs.*) This way at least we might rediscover our locked-away desire.

Jeni   Desire? I lost mine twenty years ago in a pile of dirty nappies. And I haven't the foggiest idea where it could be.

Edward   That's what we are here to search for.

Jeni   But what if it's gone for good? What if I threw it away when we bought disposables? Or perhaps the twins took it with them when they left home. God knows they took everything else. It might have been different if I was surrounded by hot-blooded students who wanted more of me than my extraordinary ability to iron pleats.

Edward   I swear to you, I have never so much as touched –

Jeni   I know. But . . .

Edward   Do you think sex is a crime? Secrecy, infidelity, hypocrisy, yes, but sex itself? Once upon a time we even used to enjoy it. Didn't we?

Jeni (*pauses*)   You've got paint on your T-shirt.

Edward   Shows I'm a painter.

Jeni   If I get egg on my dress, does that make me a chicken? I don't want to pretend to be some kid book illustrator. Why can't I just admit to being the boring wife of an art historian?

Edward   If your husband wants to become vice-chancellor he can ill afford any potential embarrassment.

Silence. The doorbell chimes.

Jeni   Leave it. Jehovah's Witnesses. They'll only want to watch.

Edward   I'm as nervous as you are.

Jeni   But you know what you want. Don't you, Edward?

The doorbell chimes again. **Edward** *rises and exits.*

Jeni   What do I do now? Should I lean languorously against the . . . or lounge lasciviously on the . . . Oh, God, the last time I did anything remotely like this I was wearing a kaftan and beads and I believed him when he said he'd just popped round to read my Tarot. He certainly didn't predict this in my future. (*Pause.*) Would I have married him if he had?

Emma (*early thirties, attractive, in expensive quilted snow jacket*) *enters. She carries a large shoulder bag under her arm and executive briefcase. She's followed by her partner* **Tony** *loaded down by a giant rucksack.* **Edward** *ushers them in.*

Edward   This is my wife, Jeni. I'm Edward.

Emma   Emma.

Tony   Tony.

Jeni   Evening.

Emma   Remarkable house.

Edward   Victorian folly. Strong Pre-Raphaelite presence here. The rumour is –

Jeni   It's not ours. National Trust. Not a fortune for a weekend out of season. I mean, frankly, wanting to rent a cottage in the Lake District in the middle of winter you'd have to be stark naked.

Edward   Stark raving, dear.

Jeni   What?

Emma   And are you?

Jeni   I'm coming reluctantly to that conclusion. A drink? Cognac to thaw you out?

Emma   Small.

Edward (*as* **Jeni** *pours her a drink, and tops herself up*)   Go steady.

Jeni   Tony?

Tony   I'm fine.

Emma   Are we the first?

Edward   Someone has to be.

Emma   Yes.

Silence.

Jeni   Would you care for a vol-au-vent, Tony?

Tony   No, thank you.

Edward   May I take your coat?

Emma   Thank you.

Edward   And your bag?

Emma   I'll hold on to that for a bit.

Edward   A lady's comfort blanket?

Emma   Exactly.

She takes off her coat to reveal an elegant scarlet gown.

Jeni   Beautiful dress.

Emma   Thank you.

Silence.

Edward   I'm afraid they are predicting more snow.

Jeni   Predictions can be wrong though, can't they?

Edward   Car managed the hill all right?

Tony   Just. (*Pause.*) Do you have chains?

Edward (*panicking*)   Chains?

Tony   For your car. Very useful in this kind of situation.

Edward   Oh, yes, that's true. Very true. (*Pauses.*) They use them a lot in Canada, I believe.

Tony   And in Scandinavia.

Edward   Yes, I would imagine . . .

Silence.

Jeni   So this is your first time as well, is it?

Emma   In the Lake District?

Jeni   No, at . . . You're swinging blue jean beginners like us?

Emma   Yes.

Jeni   That's a comfort. Blanket. We all need . . .

Emma   Yes, we do.

Edward   At least we have Shirley and Jimmy to show us the ropes. Well, not ropes. Figure of speech. And there is the swingers' code we've all signed up to, can't be coerced into anything but on the other hand permitted a kind of licence to . . . Very much brings to mind Rabelais. His Abbey of Thelema. A medieval monastery-cum-brothel-cum . . . A place where, well, in fact, written over the door was the very legend: Do What Thou Wilt is the Whole Law. Wilt of course is not wilt as in wilting. Quite the opposite. Indeed, Thelema is in fact the Greek word for will or desire.

Emma   Fascinating.

Edward   Isn't it?

Tony   Is that round here then?

Edward   What?

Tony   This monastery.

Edward   No, no, it didn't really exist. He imagined it.

Silence.

Jeni   Have you two been together long?

Emma   No.

Tony (*simultaneous*)   Yes. Time's relative, isn't it?

Jeni   Unless it's eternity.

Emma Strictly speaking we're not together, in the sense that you two are. We only meet for sex.

Jeni That is different. We only meet for breakfast.

Edward How do you mean, you only –

Emma We know nothing about each other's lives. And we ask no questions.

Jeni Never? (*To* **Tony**.) You're not just a teeny little bit curious whether she's married or –

Tony No.

Emma It would complicate everything.

Jeni But what if you fall in love?

Emma The only place we fall into is bed. That's its freedom.

Edward I can see that.

Jeni Can you?

Edward Oh, yes.

Jeni So how did you get together?

Emma The same way as here – the magic of the anonymous Internet. And then a carefully arranged rendezvous at a railway station. We had a restaurant and a hotel booked on the off chance. (*Smiling.*) We only just made it to the car park. Lust at first sight. Frankly, I hardly had time to get my knickers off.

Edward The classic zipless, eh?

Emma Exactly.

Edward Fantastic.

Emma It was.

Jeni You didn't find it a bit cramped?

Tony It was a big car.

Jeni   Oh, yes, well, it would have to be but . . . Wasn't it rather dangerous? I mean, couldn't people have seen you?

Edward   That's half the fun, isn't it?

Jeni   Is it?

Emma   We're rather into making love in dangerous places, aren't we, Tony?

Tony   Absolutely.

Edward   Like where?

Emma   Anywhere. Lifts. Shop doorways. Trains. Planes.

Edward   Mile high club.

Tony   Buses.

Emma   Woods. Fields. Beaches.

Tony   Lay-bys. Libraries. Cinemas. Swimming pools. Snooker halls. Telephone boxes. Car wash, churches –

Emma   I think they've got the picture, Tony.

Edward   Oh, yes. And you've never been caught?

Emma   Caught, no.

Tony   Watched, perhaps.

Edward   But that added to the pleasure?

Emma   Somewhat.

Jeni   Telephone box?

Tony   The old red ones.

Jeni   Oh, yes, of course, I see now. Clearly. (*Quietly.*) Excuse me. Need more ice.

She leaves.

Edward   So in a way this is really rather a natural progression for you two. A chance to spread your . . . er . . . wings . . .

Emma Perhaps. That's the experiment, isn't it?

Edward Nothing ventured. Nothing gained.

Emma So true.

Edward Isn't it? Isn't it? Hm. (*Sighs.*) Oh, sorry. Coats. Tony?

Tony *hands him his.*

Tony Thank you.

Edward Shan't be a minute. Make yourselves at home.

He exits. **Tony** *stares at* **Emma**.

Emma Problem?

Tony What was all that stuff about? We've never done anything like that in the back of a car.

Emma *is moving around with her briefcase and bag.*

Emma That's because we're married. Married folk don't.

As **Tony** *at speed begins to unload his rucksack.*

Tony So where did the idea come from?

Emma I made it up.

Tony Very impressive.

Emma I was an actress once, remember. Until reality took over.

Tony Maybe we should give it a try?

Emma We don't have a big car. Right now, we're lucky to have a car at all. Come on, there's not much time.

Tony Your briefcase down there. For wide shot. I'll cover from the door.

Tony *takes out a tiny camera from his rucksack and hides it in the ivy.* **Emma** *positions and switches on the hidden camera in her briefcase.*

Tony   I'll try for a master shot through the steamy windows.

He opens the door to the outside and nearly gets blown away in the icy blast.

Sod that for a game of soldiers. Too arty anyway.

He places a bewildering array of the latest 'spy' technology cameras, located in briefcase, bags, pens and tiny miniatures. One – an apparently folded umbrella – he hides in a potted plant.

Emma   Lighting's not brilliant.

Tony   With this new gear we could shoot down a coal mine.

Tony *expertly covers the room, hiding them in potted plants, and among the sculptures, quickly checking the angles.*

Emma   At least this lot won't chuck us in the canal like the boot boys of Hamburg.

Tony (*stopping*)   Shit, love, how the hell have we ended up like this – catching sad lonely fuckers with their trousers down. We're worth more than this.

Emma   Polishing the Bafta hasn't brought the pennies in.

Tony   Tell me, but . . . (*Shakes his head.*) I have trouble. A little question of integrity.

Emma   We're doing no different from any other of our docs. We didn't shoot up heroin, or beat up any émigrés, we just had to make it look like we did. Same here. We know what we want – we get it and we make our apologies, terribly sorry, both got a sudden migraine, and we fuck off. So what's new? (*She carefully plugs in an earpiece under her long hair.*) Everything switched on?

Tony   Should be working on satellite right now.

Emma   Sound?

Tony   On max.

Emma Paul. Can you hear me? Are you there? (*To* **Tony**.) I'm getting nothing.

Tony Control van's probably under an avalanche. Let me check the power pack.

He comes up to her and adjusts it hidden in her bra.

Emma Paul? Paul? Yes? Got you.

As **Jeni** *enters with a tray of ice.* **Emma** *grabs* **Tony** *against her breast and moans.*

Jeni (*embarrassed*) Sausages. Aga.

She turns and leaves.

Tony What was that, my Christmas treat?

Emma Paul's asking if everything's ready.

Tony Nearly. Figure most of the action will be here, but I'll get some basic cover in the other rooms.

Emma (*to* **Paul**) We're practically ready to go. (*To* **Tony**.) They're all set his end.

Tony Five minutes.

He stares at her.

Emma It's not the end of the line, Tony, it's the beginning. We need this to kick the ratings off. After that, we're back on the road looking for the real bad boys.

Tony Pack 'em in with presents, then preach. Gospel according to St Paul.

Emma He happens to be right. So let's get it over with and out.

Tony (*sighs*) Right.

Carrying his rucksack he moves to the conservatory door as **Jeni** *reappears.*

Jeni Sausage?

Tony   Bathroom, love?

Jeni   Straight down the hall.

Emma (*downstage, whispering*)   Yes, human interest. Start. Trust me.

Tony *exits.* **Emma** *strokes down her dress.* **Jeni** *waves the tray of sausages at her.*

Jeni   Sausage?

Emma   Not right now, thank you.

Jeni   May I ask you a question?

Emma   Of course.

Jeni   How do you manage to keep it on the ball, boil, keep it on the boil?

Emma   By making sure it's separate from real life.

Jeni   But is it?

Emma   Absolutely. Real life is mundane by definition. Boring. Passion is going to the pictures. You enter into its world and start to glow in the dark. Life's a documentary, but this is a film, a fiction. And fun. If you don't like it you can just walk out. That's not quite so easy in real life.

Jeni   I love films. I spend all day watching old movies. Even thought about taking up smoking because it seems so sexy. They never cough, do they?

Emma   That's what I'm saying. Not real.

Jeni   But don't you sometimes want to bring it into real life?

Emma (*pauses*)   It's a temptation.

The doorbell chimes.

Jeni (*paying no attention*)   Do you think Tony would fancy me? It doesn't matter, of course, if he doesn't. I'd understand perfectly.

Emma Do you fancy him?

Jeni I should have made some dips. I normally do. I just forgot.

Jimmy (*late thirties, northern, working class, fast-talking*) *slams his way through* **Jack**'s *door, carrying cardboard boxes. He's followed by his wife* **Shirley**, *hidden under her cagoule.* **Edward** *follows, staggering under cardboard boxes.*

Jimmy (*impressed*) Bloody hell, Shirl, get this. You could take your holidays in here if they serve lager.

Jeni Evening.

Jimmy (*staring at the stained glass*) And a flash muriel as well. I love that kind of thing wi' the light behind. We've done it with fish and it looks fab. They're a lovely a pair aren't they? (*Grinning.*) And he's well provided an' all.

Edward Actually, it's almost certainly a Rossetti.

Jimmy Yeh, well, I'd expect an award if I had one that size.

Edward No, I meant –

Jimmy Drop 'em.

Edward What?

Jimmy Next load, sunshine.

Edward You're not really serious about unpacking the whole of your van?

Jimmy Never know what you might need to get the party going. Be prepared.

Shirley Jimmy were a Boy Scout before he were a sex-maniac.

Jimmy (*as he sorts out the boxes*) Tenth commandment: 'A scout shall be clean in thought, word and deed.' Honest, now – possible you might manage the word and deed bit for a couple of weeks, but who can stop the thoughts, eh? And if you've got the thought, well, apparently, according to the knock-kneed scoutmaster you're fucked anyway, so you might as well go for the deed, and if you do the dirty deed then what's so wrong with using the right words? Just hypocrisy not to. Call a spade a spade, and a cock a cock, that way you don't get confused and try digging up your sprouts with your plonker. (*To* **Edward**.) Come on, mate, give us a hand. No sexual innuendo implied.

Edward   Pardon?

Jimmy   You know what I mean, that kind of thing between men, whole different ball park, not that I'm judging them.

And he's gone. A stunned **Edward** *follows. Silence.*

Shirley   I'm not going to apologise for my husband. I've done enough by marrying him.

She lets down the cagoule hood. She's late thirties, attractive without being either brash or stunning, with an open demeanor.

Shirley   I'm Shirley.

Jeni   Jeni.

Emma   Emma.

Shirley   Lovely names. I were called after Shirley Eaton. She got covered in gold paint in *Goldfinger*. Me dad were a painter.

Emma   Portraits?

Shirley   Whitewash and walls. (*To* **Emma**, *simply*.) You look a picture yourself.

Emma   Thank you.

Jeni   Would you care for a drink, Shirley?

Shirley   Got Martini?

Jeni   Oh.

Shirley   Don't fret. Nobody ever has so I've brought my own. (*Takes out a large bottle.*) Glass would be grand but not essential.

Emma   Might I have a top up?

As **Jeni** *sorts out the drinks.*

Shirley   Fantastic this. Woun't credit it were snowing outside. Brilliant. Always amazes me –

Emma   Snow?

Shirley   No, life. You go through one door and you're in one world, walk through another and you're in a completely different one t'other.

Emma   I gather from your website you and your husband have walked through quite a few doors?

Shirley   Well, it's our hobby. 'Bout the only thing we share. I don't play golf, and he dun't do bingo.

Emma   Is it a hobby you ever pursue separately?

Shirley   We're a good married couple. White wedding, full vows. We'd have had a bishop for the service if he an't had diarrhoea.

Emma   So what made you take up this?

Shirley   Let's be honest, duck, I don't think none of us couples'd be here if we answered everything for each other. I'm not even sure that's possible for anybody. P'raps folks just kid themselves.

Jeni   You think two people can't just love each other?

Shirley   I won't talking about love. Just saying they can't answer every need, like. Try as they might. Anyroad we coun't.

Jeni   I didn't mean to pry.

Shirley   That's all right, petal. Part of livin' and learnin'.

She takes off the cagoule to reveal a tight-fitting dress.

Shirley   Me and Jimmy wanted kids real bad but . . . tried the works but it din't turn out, took us into a bad patch did that. All time planners and thermometers and I didn't feel particularly sexy and for Jimmy it come more of a duty than a delight. (*Smiles.*) Anyroad, first bloke what come along and fancied me after that, nothing else, just fancied me, well it . . . I din't see it coming, it just took me by surprise, like walking in out the cold into a steamin' bath. There's nought beats being fancied.

Jeni   Isn't there?

Shirley   Ace. I loved it, and the same time I felt bloody awful.

Emma   Some folk get a thrill out of the deceit.

Shirley   Not me. I hated the lying.

As **Jimmy** *returns, with* **Edward** *bent under more boxes.*

Jimmy   Can't find the air pump for Claudia.

Shirley   Lent it to Val for the kids' balloons.

Jimmy (*wryly*)   There goes me vent act then.

Shirley   It's his party piece.

Edward   What a disappointment.

Jimmy (*grinning*)   You don't mean that, do you? Emma. Jeni. Got you. Now then, in these boxes are the board games. Can be useful for getting party loosened up, like.

Edward   We get to play Monopoly?

Jimmy   Sexopoly. The Community Chest really lives up to its name.

Tony *enters. He gives the nod to* **Emma**.

Jeni   Found the bathroom OK?

Tony   No problem.

Jimmy Tony, eh? Shirl here picked you out personally. Lucky, cos there's a big waiting list for these beginners' nights, you know.

Tony I'm flattered.

Emma (*softly*) We're running.

Shirley (*smiles to* **Jimmy**) I were just telling the girls here about Wally.

Jimmy (*nods, not bothered*) Oh, right.

Emma Human interest section.

Tony Who's Wally?

Jimmy (*as he sorts out his gear*) Shirl had a fling a while back. Before we got into this malarkey. I went berserk, and lost use of me three-piece suite all at the same time.

Edward Your what?

Jimmy Went on the dip, me old fruit. Foaming with fury and fuckin' impotent. Would have been a classic cock-up if it hadn't been the exact bloody opposite. We should label these boxes, pet.

Tony So how did you . . . er . . .

Jimmy Get back on the job with a rise? Not easy, mate. Problem with that soddin' thought thing up here. I coun't get him and her out me head, picturing it from first fumble to final fuck, replaying it like some bleedin' *Nightmare on Elm Street* movie. Course she swore she an't enjoyed it for a sec, but I din't believe her.

Shirley Said I were no good at lying.

Jimmy I still loved her, in and among wanting her dead and served up as salad with his sliced salami, but seeing her getting her rocks off with . . .

Tony Did you know the man?

Jimmy   Just to make it worse. He were our gardener. Part-time. Rest of the time he were fuckin' her. And charging me by the hour.

Shirley   Exaggeration, Jimmy. Anyway, I ditched him dead quick.

Jimmy   Oh, aye, she stayed with me, like, she loved me, I knew that, but it blew me confidence out. I coun't trust her. Every time she went on the bus into town I pictured her gi'ing the conductor a blow-job cos she din't have the right change.

Shirley   He just went on and on about it.

Jeni   You should have got her a bus pass.

Edward   Jeni.

Jimmy (*smiling as he unloads various vibrators, sex-toys*)   I were over the hill and far away with the fairies, the proper fairies not . . . Making up pictures like you coun't credit, Postman Pat gets a packet, milkman doles out extra cream, it was like I were trapped in two bleedin' worlds at the same time. I played five-a-side football and I'd be in the shower and I'd reach me for me towel and see her gi'in the boys more than a slice of orange. And then the ref. And the linesmen. Then she'd start on the fucking away team. Played havoc with me game. I were goal-keeper. Bloody important job, but there's time for your mind to wander. Then I were standing there one Sunday, and I suddenly twigged as I saw her down on her knees givin' assistance to a bloke in the penalty area that I had got a fuckin' hard on. Bit tricky when you're wearing a box but . . . It were a shock. Never saw the winning ball. Bloody unnerving when your nightmare turns into your fantasy. Din't know what to feel – we lost the league but I got me mojo working. And I twigged then it were working for me as long as I imagined I were there, as long as it were something we had planned together. So she didn't have to hide away and betray me. Still made me sweat. I kept the thought to myself for a long time, then –

Shirley   He finally confessed.

Tony   That he wanted to watch?

Shirley   Yeh.

Jeni   How did you feel?

Shirley   Well, I were a bit taken back at first. Woun't you be?

Jeni   Yes.

Shirley   But he wanted to face it.

Edward   Thought, word and deed.

Jimmy   Aye, but the deed took a length of time.

Shirley (*taking his hand*)   And a lot of guts.

Emma   And how did you feel?

Shirley   It were me at fault. And I loved him. I were game.

Jimmy   Say that again.

Shirley   Not that first time by a long chalk. I were shakin' like a leaf. Met the man in a hotel, din't we? We'd cleared it all like on the Internet, what we wanted. Still . . .

Tony   And?

Shirley   Well, it were OK like. He were a nice enough bloke.

Emma   Did you orgasm?

Shirley   Not first time, no.

Tony (*to* **Jimmy**)   But when she did, where were you?

Jimmy   I were holding her hand. It were grand.

Tony   So you don't mind her going off with other fellows?

Jimmy   *Au contraire*, pal. I hate it.

Tony   I don't follow.

Jimmy   I coun't cope wi' her copping off wi'out me, that'd set all them nightmare movies off again. *Nightmare on Elm Street*, episode sixty-nine.

Shirley   I've never wanted to, anyway.

Jimmy   We don't hold truck wi' that seventies wife-swapping throw the car keys in the middle of the coffee-table and bunk off to separate bedrooms ballocks. Not saying, however, if you some of you want that just to get you revved up, up to you, but it in't for me and Shirl. Our one golden rule. Those who fuck together, stay stuck together.

Jeni   There's a picture.

Edward   And it doesn't bother you, others watching her as well?

Jimmy   I'm proud of my missis. She's a great little performer. Camera loves her.

Tony   Camera?

Emma   You an actress?

Shirley   Amateur.

Jimmy   Cheap camcord. Just a private memento for us.

Emma   You take it very seriously.

Jimmy   Well, I sketch out a few scenes. What the pros call scenarios. I do a little storyboard sometimes, pictures of stick men with three legs. Learnt it from a book on 'itchcock.

Edward   Not so much the itch, more the cock.

Jimmy   He's a wit your husband, in't he?

Jeni   And do you . . . in the films . . . Do you not leave anything to the imagination?

Jimmy   It has to be for real. It's hard core. Whole point is revealing what them above have forbidden us to see. You ever seen a porno film?

Jeni   Well, years ago, we went to see Marlon Brando in *Last Tango in Paris*.

Jimmy   Crap that is. All that does is put you off butter.

Edward   It's a Bertolucci.

Jimmy   It's a pain in the arse.

Edward   So what kind of brilliant 'scenarios' do you do then?

Jimmy   I make no claims. I'm not up for an Oscar. Though Shirl is if you know somebody of that name. No, they're just basic. Well, they're supposed to be, aren't they? Classic example – 'In a Spin'.

Shirley (*singing*)   'Oh, what a spin I'm in.'

Jimmy   Bored housewife, spin-dryer bust, in comes the plumber with his adjustable spanner.

Shirley   He won't really a plumber.

Jimmy   And the spin-dryer won't really broke, but that's film, in't it? You mek it up. Mind you, the moment he plugged in, and started the full cycle with you sat on it, stone me . . . Not a dry seat in the house. Got me goin'. I tend to fuck the story up by havin' to join in, but there you go. I cover up best I can – shocked husband who's then finally sucked in.

Jeni   So you have . . . with two men at the same time? So what's that like?

Shirley   Can be a bit bewildering at first, you just can't tell where it's coming from next. But once you settle in, it's lovely, actually. Hard work but worth it in the long run.

Edward (*to* **Jimmy**)   And do you have sex with the man?

Jimmy (*shocked*)   Edward, Edward, you're not trying to come it wi' me, are you?

Emma   What about you with other women?

Shirley   Yes.

Emma   And how does that feel?

Shirley (*smiles*)   Different. Light. As opposed to dark. Like in chocolate.

Edward   And do you sometimes join in with that?

Jimmy   Once in a blue moon. The lasses tend to be very preoccupied. But to be honest, I'm as happy watching.

Shirley (*to* **Emma**)   Are you OK with a woman?

Emma   Not really my scene.

Shirley   Jeni?

Jeni   I hadn't really thought . . . I don't think I've ever really . . . No, truth is I did have a crush on one of the prefects at boarding school. Cynthia Henderson. We shared a hairbrush once.

Edward   What?

Jeni   But it came to nothing. She was in love with the French assistant, Mam'selle LaRoche. As were we all.

Edward   You never mentioned.

Jeni   What about you? Did prep pep you up?

Edward (*shrugs*)   I'm not denying a certain mutual pleasuring. It's a phase one goes through. Segregated sexes. What else can one expect?

Jeni   You don't think we could all be bisexual, then?

Edward   That's just a theory.

Jeni   And how would one test it?

Jimmy   Hold on, there. Rule two of swingtime – not everything is up for grabs. Well, not by everybody. Right, come on, party time! These here are the costume boxes.

Edward   Costumes?

Jimmy   Dressing up's magic. Soon as you think you're somebody else, you'll fucking amaze yourself. Believe me.

Shirley   Like me in them films. I woun't have done half those things in real life.

Emma   But you did.

Shirley   Wasn't me. It were character I were playing.

Emma   Fine line.

Shirley   Not once you've crossed it.

Jimmy   Crossing the line, that's what we're here to do.

Edward   Transgression.

Jeni *throws him a look.*

Jimmy   OK, first volunteer. (*To* **Jeni**.) Now then, sweetheart, what you got to lose?

Jeni   I've no idea. What you got?

Jimmy   Most of this stuff's from Shirl's musical society.

Shirley   We went bust staging *Cats*.

Jimmy   We din't get them cossies, though. So you can't be that kind of hot little pussy.

Shirley   Could do you a nice French maid's outfit from *The Boyfriend*. Or a tart from *Irma La Douce*.

Jeni   Shirley Maclaine. One of my favourites. Do I get a beret as well?

Shirley   Somewhere.

Edward   Jeni.

Jeni   Isn't this what we are here for, Edward?

Jimmy   That's the spirit. So, me old fruit, what kind of musical are you into?

Edward   I prefer opera.

Jimmy   Well, we 'aven't got Wagner's Ring and if we had you woun't really want to play wi' it, would you?

Edward   I find your innuendos really distasteful.

Shirley   Stop it, Jimmy.

Jimmy   Sorry, mate.

Jeni (*rooting around in the boxes*)   Ah, here you go, Edward. Perfect.

She holds up a schoolmaster's gown, over an old three-piece grey flannel suit.

Shirley   *Goodbye Mr Chips*. Broke my heart did that.

Jeni   I preferred the original film version. Robert Donat in black and white. Come on, Edward, you'll look good in it. You know, he's always secretly rather fancied himself as a professor.

Jimmy   Secret fantasies – the name of the game.

Jeni   And a mortar to boot.

Edward   Is this strictly necessary?

Jeni   Don't be a party poop, Edward.

Edward *takes it with great reluctance.*

Jimmy   Tony, what about you, sunshine ? I see you as a natural Curly but I'm only guessin'.

Tony   I beg your pardon?

Jimmy *holds up a cowboy hat.*

Jimmy   Curly. The cowboy. 'Oh, what a beautiful . . .' *Oklahoma*.

Shirley   'I'm just a girl who can't say no.'

Jimmy   And that's straight from the horse's mouth.

Shirley   Come on, Tony.

Jimmy (*holding up the 'chaps'*)   Just make sure the chaps don't rub together. Know what I mean?

Tony   Not me. Really.

Jimmy   *Camelot.* Lancelot? Or is that just a tempting rumour?

Shirley   I've the very thing.

She holds up a doctor's gown.

Jeni   What musical has a doctor in it?

Jimmy   One from our private collection. Doctors. Nurses. Vicars.

Shirley   Some costumes you just have to have.

Edward   The classic archetypes.

Emma   Male fantasies.

Shirley   And women's. Like this one.

Jimmy   She goes weak at the knees for a man with a nice stethoscope.

Shirley   You know you're safe in their hands, don't you? Come on, Tony.

Tony *glances at* **Emma**. *She shrugs.*

Tony   So what you going to wear, Emma?

Jimmy   I rather fancy you in *Grease* – and I mean that quite literally.

Emma   Oh. I'm not really into –

Tony   It's just a little improvisation, sweetheart. You're good at that.

Jimmy (*digging out the nurse's outfit*)   Doctors and nurses. *Voilà!*

Shirley   I don't know, Jimmy.

Jimmy   Don't panic. I'll make sure they're not stuck on the same ward together. Come on, duck.

Emma *tilts her head, listening, then sighs.*

Emma   OK.

Shirley   We din't bring underwear. I think folk feel more at home in their own.

Jeni   Yes.

Jimmy   Although it's amazing how keen they are to get into somebody else's. And now what are you going to wear, your little classic black number? The old standby, so to speak? (*He holds up a nun's habit.*) 'How do you solve a problem like Maria?'

Shirley   'How do you hold a moonbeam in your hand?'

Jeni   Is nothing sacred?

Shirley   Are you religious as well?

Jeni   I am about Julie Andrews. (*She suddenly bursts into a fit of giggles.*) Sorry. Sorry.

Jeni *pours herself another drink.*

Emma   And what you wearing, Jimmy?

Jimmy *holds up a sarong as, with varying degrees of willingness, they begin to undress.*

Jimmy   Guess.

Jeni   Bloody Mary in *South Pacific*?

Jimmy   Not bloody likely.

Jeni   Audrey Hepburn in *My Fair Lady*?

Jimmy   Don't be daft. It's *The King and I.*

Edward   Shouldn't it be crinoline, then?

Jimmy   I'm the king! It's one of them sarong things.

Jeni   'It's the sarong time, it's the sarong place.'

Edward   Don't catch his disease.

Jimmy   Hold on there, mate. I'm as clean as a whistle.

Edward   No, I meant the compulsion to pun –

Jimmy   Go on, check your pocket. Abracadabra. (*As* **Edward** *takes out the condom packets.*) Bugger me, party balloons. You can either blow 'em up, or stick 'em over something that's already inflated. Safe sex, sunshine. All the outfits have a selection. No self-respecting nun would go down on her knees without a three-pack, would she, sister?

Shirley   Golden rule.

Jimmy (*to* **Jeni**)   Yours are in your bag. And Tony and our nurse have a full supply. Them being medics an' all. Mine I keep in my pouch.

Shirley *shimmies out of her dress to reveal the basque underneath.* **Tony** *is by her side. She smiles.* **Jimmy** *leans over* **Tony**'*s shoulder.*

Jimmy   Got your first patient already. Say 'Big breaths, my dear'. Go on.

Tony   Wha' . . . Er . . . 'Big breaths, my dear.'

Shirley (*laughing, lisping*)   'Yeth, doctor, and I'm only thixteen'.

Jimmy *laughs.* **Tony** *is totally lost.*

Jimmy   It's an old seaside postcard gag.

Shirley   That's where Jimmy learned everything he knows about sex.

Edward   That hardly comes as a surprise.

Jimmy   Oh, so what did you learn the secrets of life from?

Edward (*pauses*)   *Lady Chatterley's Lover.*

Jimmy   And what did she have to say about that? Was she understanding?

Edward   Actually, it's a book.

Jimmy   Really? (*Insulted.*) Bugger me. It's a book.

Jimmy *starts to strip near* **Jeni** *who is half-hiding behind a plant. This doesn't bother* **Jimmy**. **Tony** *is about to put on his medical coat.*

Shirley   You need to take your shirt off. They only wear a vest in *ER*. It gets very hot on the wards.

Downstage: **Emma** *struggling with her mike as she tries to get in her nurse's outfit.*

Emma (*whispering*)   Paul? I'm trying. Just don't want to lose you.

Tony *starts to take off his shirt.* **Jimmy** *now in underpants and socks, watching* **Jeni** *put on fishnet stockings.* **Edward** *proprietorially nearby.*

Jimmy   You've kept well there.

Jeni   Low mileage. One careful owner. Service twice a year.

Edward   It's been more than that.

Jeni   Oh, yeh. Plus the annual MOT . . . (*Edgy.*) Jimmy, could you do me a favour?

Jimmy   Bothers you me looking at you?

Jeni   No, no, actually it's the socks. No socks, please, we're British.

Jimmy   Fair enough.

He turns away to watch his wife reach out to **Tony**'s *chest.*

Shirley   'Oh, doctor, I'm in trouble.'

Jimmy (*on one leg, taking his socks off*)   'Well, goodness gracious me.'

Jeni (*almost automatically*)   Sophie Loren. *The Millionairess.*

Jimmy   She had big breaths as well.

He winks at his wife and moves downstage.

Shirley   You think you might be able to help me, doctor?

Tony   Well . . . I . . . er . . .

She takes his hand and places it on her heart. He stares at her.

Shirley   Oh, my God, doctor, you're making a nun blush.

Tony   Better put your habit on then.

Shirley   Fuck the habit.

Tony   Don't give up the Church for me. I'm not worth it.

Shirley   I don't know, doctor, I think you might be.

She embraces him. He looks wildly towards **Emma** *for support. She's whispering to* **Paul**. *They slide to the ground out of view. Shadows loom large behind the stained-glass doors. They open to reveal two sodden, ice-bound figures enter,* **Jack** *and* **Jill** (*under the snow two young English roses*). **Jeni** *is the first to see them. She backs away in horror and crashes over the hidden figures of* **Tony** *and* **Shirley**.

Shirley (*voice*)   Not now, thank you!

Tony (*voice*)   No problem ! No problem!

Jimmy (*in sarong and one sock*)   Fuck me, it's the Yetis!

Jack   Evening.

Edward *steps forward with some attempt at decorum.*

Edward   Good evening. How can we . . . (*As his trousers fall down.*) Who wore this fucking outfit, Pavarotti? Terribly sorry. How can we help you?

As the others begin slowly to appear in their varying forms of dishabille.

Edward   This must look a little odd to you. Logical explanation, we're just in the middle of . . .

Jeni   Rehearsing . . .

Edward   Yes, rehearsing the school play. It's . . . (*Looks around.*) It's a new play. (*As the half-naked* **Tony** *and* **Shirley** *rise.*) Contemporary themes. Just for the upper sixth, not the lower school. So if you'll excuse us, don't want to lose the dramatic flow, you know.

Jack   No, no, of course not. Terribly sorry. Just our car broke down, and yours was the only light in the night. I wondered would you happen to know where Ecclestone Folly might be?

Edward   Why do you want there?

Jack   A party. Sort of. Event.

Jimmy   A do?

Jack   Yes, in a way, you could . . . A do.

Jimmy   Hang on, hang on a mo. You're not Jack, are you?

Jack   No.

Jill   Yes.

Jack   Yes, sorry, no, I meant yes.

Jimmy   Well, I'll go to the foot of our stairs and bugger the cat. It's Jack and Jill come up the hill. I din't have you for coming. Your last email said someowt about cancelling a choir. I coun't make head nor tail.

Jack   Oh, did it . . . ah . . .

Jimmy   No sweat, son, you're here now. Fantastic. Welcome to Paradise. I'm Jimmy, the King of Siam. The nun on the run is my missis Shirl. This here's Jeni, our resident French tart. Jeni's husband, Edward, our house-master.

Jeni   You're not really called Jack and Jill, are you?

Jimmy   No, their names have been changed to protect their innocence.

Jill   We're not that innocent.

Jack   Least, we hope not to be.

Jimmy   Doctor Tony there. And his companion nurse Emma lurking in the shadows.

Emma   Evening.

Jack   You're not really rehearsing a play?

Shirley   Just dressing up for a bit of fun. Get the party goin'.

Jack   Oh, right.

Tony (*aside*)   Why didn't you help me?

Emma   When?

Edward   I think you really should take all your clothes off straight away.

Jeni   You're a bit quick off the mark, aren't you?

Edward   I simply meant before they both catch their death of cold.

Jill   Oh, yes.

Edward   Let me help you.

They start to take off their clothes.

Jill   What an extraordinary place.

Edward   It's part Victorian Gothic combined with the nostalgic medievalism of the Pre-Raphaelites and Morris. Makes for an intensively suggestive combination, most clearly embodied in the seductive *pièce de resistance* of the triptych of the –

Jeni   Cut the lecture, headmaster. Just get the poor souls a drink.

Edward   Yes, of course. Cognac OK?

Jill   Anything. Bless you.

Jeni   He's just getting into his part.

Shirley   What's with the choir, Jack? Not into the church are you?

Jack   No, no, not at all, no, not really, no –

Emma   You don't seem quite sure.

Jack   No.

Jill   Actually we were once, weren't we? Long time ago. When we were young.

Emma *moves her handbag for a better shot of the stripping couple and nods for* **Tony** *to redirect one of his.* **Jeni** *and* **Shirley** *help folding clothes.*

Emma   Is that how you two met?

Jill   At university. Yes. We were both sick to death with the lech and lager brigade. Keen to change the world. Became newborn. Pro-life. Which meant really being anti-everything to do with sex – abortions, homosexuals, page three, promiscuity. We even took the vow of chastity until we got married.

Edward   Was that difficult?

Jack   Yes.

Jill   And it didn't really give us a lot of insight as to what to do after, either.

Jack   No.

Jimmy   So you've ended up bored rigid with the missionary number, eh?

Jill   Rather.

Jack (*confused*)   Sorry, how . . . Excuse . . . How did you know about that?

Jimmy   'Bout what?

Jack   That we were once missionaries.

Jimmy   No, I din't. I were just guessing on your sex life.

Jill   Actually, it was that experience – the missionary – that brought us to our senses, wasn't it, Jack? There we were preaching to these people that the cause of their problems wasn't poverty or the Aids plague, but their own lack of purity. All they had to do was turn back to righteousness and prayer. And of course renounce the last small solace that one human being can offer another. We wanted them to be what we imagined we were – angels in hell. I burn with shame even now to think that I believed . . .

Jack takes her hand.

Edward   You're not alone, Jill. We're all a product of the Church's two-thousand-year attack on sexual desire. It left no stone unturned. What other religion had to turn a mother into a virgin.

Shirley (*now dressed as a nun*)   But why would it do that?

Jimmy   I can see a spiritual crisis coming on here, sister.

Edward   Fear of losing control.

Jack   It was the Church Leaders, more perhaps than the true teachings of the Lord.

Jimmy   Them knock-kneed scoutmasters?

Edward   So you discover pro-life is anti – and the missionary position is far too limiting, and now the two of you are here determined to break through that cruel judgement imposed on our basic humanity. To escape its sentence, to become truly free. To discover the sensual life itself in all its richness and potency.

Jack   Well, I suppose . . . I wouldn't have used . . . But . . .

Edward (*to Jill*)   And you understand that journey means stepping out into the totally unknown?

Jill   Yes.

She stands naked. She smiles at him. Silence.

Jeni   Give them the sodding drinks, Edward!

Edward   Ah, sorry.

He hands them the drinks. The scene looks like a modern version of Déjeuner sur l'Herbe. *Silence.* **Emma** *is nodding, smiling.* (**Paul** *is pleased.*) *She grins at* **Tony**. **Shirley** *beams benignly at the young couple.*

Jeni   We really ought to find you some clothes to wear.

Jill   Don't worry. We're quite used to being naked with people. We went on a nudist holiday in the south of France.

Emma   And was that sexually liberating?

Jack   It was very pleasant but not quite what we imagined. The French take their grandparents with them on holiday.

Jimmy   God, you'd think the frogs would have more taste, woun't you? After all it's the race what gave the world *soixante-neuf.* Fuck knows what most of us did before that.

Edward (*to* **Jill**)   Still, I imagine you got plenty of fresh air. And exercise. You're obviously in excellent shape.

Jill   A little ping-pong, that's all. Oh, and Jack made the volleyball team.

Shirley   Was that fun?

Jack   Actually it was quite painful.

Jeni (*holding up a schoolgirl's gymslip*)   The very thing for you, Jill.

Jill   It's not very sexy.

Jeni   There's those who'd disagree, aren't there, Edward?

Edward   Is this your fantasy or mine?

Jeni   I can't tell any more. Is that part of my problem?

Shirley   Go on, love, half the fun is taking them off again.

Jill   Well, you're the leaders.

Emma (*aside*)   Paul loves this.

Tony   I bet.

Jimmy (*digging out the costume*)   And for Jack – Jesus Christ Superstar! Perfect.

Jack   Jesus? I'm not sure. I know I was . . . And we talk of the Church and . . . but for me, you see, I don't really see Jesus as the problem so much as . . . So I'm not really sure that I could . . . you know . . . As . . . Not quite ready.

Jimmy   Wha's matter? Scared of being struck by lightning?

The sudden thunder of falling snow.

Tony   Or an avalanche?

Jimmy (*pauses*)   Well maybe not Jesus. But we might get away with the classic vicar number.

Jack   I'd really prefer not –

Shirley   I rather fancy you as a man of the cloth.

Edward   The classic image. The repressed cleric breaking through. Hawthorne. Think of *The Scarlet Letter*.

Jimmy   Or whatever colour condom turns you on, sunshine!

Jack *looks at* **Jill** *and then relents.* **Edward** *settles down by* **Jill** *with his light controls, clearly bent on giving her the most sensitive lights.* **Jack** *dresses up in the dog collar.*

Edward   So what was your next step on the path to excess?

Jill   We joined a witches' coven. Another waste of time. All they did was make us hug trees.

Jack   Actually I was lucky there. I got quite a nice tree.

Jill   Apart from the splinter.

Jack   Well, yes, true.

Jill   Everywhere we tried, everything was sanitised. All disembodied spirit or purgings and purity. Terrified ultimately of sex. That's why when we found your site, it was refreshing, at least you were being honest. Genuinely non-judgemental about sexuality. Nothing to be guilty about, everything to be explored.

Edward (*to* **Jack**)   And perhaps even your Jesus would have agreed with that.

Jack   Pardon?

Edward   You know about the early Christian sects?

Jimmy   I do.

Edward   Really?

Jimmy   Sure. Early Christian sex. It's a nun giving head before breakfast.

Shirley   Jimmy, folk are trying to be serious here.

Jimmy   Why?

Edward   I was referring to those groups celebrating Agape.

Jimmy   A – what?

Jack   Agape. It means love-feast. (*Nodding.*) It was apparently very common in the early days of the faith.

Edward   You've done your homework. There are some scholars who argue it was much more than a mere feast. That it drew from the fertility rites of the ancient Eleusinian mysteries, the Dionysian debauch, the Roman bacchanal. Communal transgression. The sheer force to transform of the orgy. Of course, the life-haters, Saint Paul and his merry men, damned the participants as heretics and they were driven deep underground. Literally. Into the dark night of

the catacombs. And perhaps they're still there – repressed
but not finally beaten – sending up strange coded messages
and images across history: graffiti on the walls of the caves,
pornography run off on Gutenberg's printing press, stained-
glass windows posing as purity and secretly postulating
passion, signs and wonders for those who know how to read
it, and, who knows, perhaps even we are part of this
movement without realising it, as we grope in the dark of
the dungeons of desire . . . Perhaps we here now, perhaps
we are unconsciously the true searchers for Agape and all
we need to bring to the feast is the courage to transgress.

Jeni (*quietly*)   Chapter two.

A stunned silence. **Jill** *slowly nods.* **Jack** *follows suit.*

Jimmy   I don't have the foggiest what the fuck you are
talking about, but if it's a sex feast you're after, ding-dong
your balls are ringing because you've come to the right
place. Welcome, friends, to the bistro of bonking. And on
the menu for your delight is – sex, lots of different choices,
courses, from a bit of hanky-panky *hors d'oeuvre* to a
quivering blancmange for dessert, but the point is, fair
enough, nobody has to eat any more than they want to, and
some of us might be quite happy to sit back and simply do a
bit of serving up, who knows, it's not school dinners,
nobody's going to rap you over the back of your hand with a
hot spoon if you decide to skip the meat dish but I will tell
you this much, there's not much point being here if you
don't at least want to stick your tongue in a vol-au-vent.
Right then, who's up for starters?

Jack   Forgive me. It just seems a little . . .

Jimmy   What?

Jack   I don't know exactly. Just perhaps a trifle . . .

Edward   Crude?

Jack   Possibly.

Jimmy   That's the point. It's a trifle crude, a crude trifle.
Try it back to front it comes to the same thing. Literally. I
know, you want to talk about love. Course you do. You're a
vicar. Good for you. Now, whatever you say about love, and
I'm a great believer in it, I'm allers shinning up and down
high walls bringing Shirl boxes of Milk Tray, but the
unchangeable fact is it's not love but sex that makes the
world go round, and sex doesn't always have to be wrapped
up in ribbons or clingfilm, although sometimes that can be
fun as well, and there's the key word to a successful orgy.
Fun. Sex is entertainment. Showbiz. Show time! A slap and
a tickle. Nudge nudge, wink wink. Audience participation.
Join in the chorus. By Christ, don't we all need a laugh now
and then in this bloody day and age, eh, vicar?

Edward   I think we all rather hoped it might be a little
more meaningful than just a bit of a laugh.

Jimmy   Laughing don't make an experience any less
important. We laughed on our honeymoon, didn't we,
petal?

Shirley   Well, I did.

Jimmy   So come on, then, step right up. First served, first
come.

Edward   Oh really.

Jeni   Oh, don't play games, headmaster. You've been
drooling over the starters since she arrived.

Edward   I don't know what you are talking about.

Jeni (*to* **Jill**, *with a French accent*)   Eh, *attention*, Mam'selle
Henderson. I zink the headmaster has want of you in his
bureau study.

Jill   What . . . Who are you?

Jeni   *Sacre bleu!* I'm Mam'selle LaRoche, zee French
mistress, for Christ's sake! Pay attention.

Jack   Oh, it's a game. A charade?

Jeni   You may call it that but it's life or death, *la vie où la mort*, to some of us, Monsieur Chapelain.

Jack   Chaplin. I'm Charlie Chaplin?

Jeni   Chaplain. *Pour l'école.*

Jack   Right. With you. *Bien sur.*

Jeni   *Allons, ma jeune fillette.*

Jill   What have I done? Have I done something really wicked?

Jeni   The head he takes your behaviour in the shower with the football team *très sérieusement. Moi-même*, I am sure you were only trying to, how you say . . . raise their spirits, but . . . with the away team as well. Oh la la!

Jimmy   Cheeky bugger's nicking my ideas.

Jill   Oh, right. (*Pause.*) Well, had I better go then?

Jack   Well, you . . . You don't have to.

Jeni   You wish to see her expulsed, Monsieur Chapelain?

Jack   No, no, madame, of course, but . . . (*Desperately.*) It just seems to me, in my official position, here, I wonder if what she did is not really wicked, is it, I mean, she was misguidedly admittedly trying to help, to offer solace even to the . . . other side.

Jill (*quietly*)   It was wicked.

Jeni   Bravo, mam'selle. *Quel courage!*

Jill   Don't worry. I'm sure it won't be anything too serious. (*Kisses him lightly and turns away.*) I don't know the way.

Jeni   Headmaster?

Edward   Do you know what you are doing?

Jeni   Do you? You should. You've dreamt it often enough.

Edward (*pauses*)   This way, Henderson.

Jill (*to* **Jeni**)   Will you come with me?

Jeni *pauses, then slowly pushes back the girl's hair from her face.*

Jeni (*no trace of an accent*)   That is so kind of you. But the headmaster and I . . . (*Shakes her head.*) It's difficult to explain.

Edward *and* **Jill** *both leave.*

Jeni   Goodbye, Mr Chips.

Jeni, *shaking, pours herself a drink.*

Emma   Study? Covered?

Tony *nods.*

Jack   Ought I to go with her?

Jimmy   If it were me, mate, front row seat.

Jeni   Best to leave them be.

Jack *sits by the fountain.*

Jeni   You don't have the answer for what she wants. You know that, don't you? (*Sits by him.*) What do you want, Jack? (*He shakes his head.*) This wasn't your idea, was it? (*Pause.*) Well, we're both here now. Classic double act, eh?

Jack   Sorry?

Jeni   Vicar and tart.

Jack   Oh, yes, right.

Jeni (*sighs, then*)   *Pardon, monsieur, vous avez besoin d'une amie? Vous êtes anglais?* English? *Hein, je le pense.* (*She holds out a hand to him.*) You like I show you the sights?

Jack *hesitates, then stands and takes her hand. They turn towards the door.*

Jimmy   Whoa, hold on. Where you two off to?

Jeni   I zink to show him Sacre Coeur.

Jimmy Show him your sacred bleedin' coeur here, sweetheart. Come on, this is supposed to be an orgy not a two by two into the fucking ark.

Jeni Later.

Jack Yes. *Plus tard.*

Jeni and Jack leave. **Emma** *glances at* **Tony**.

Tony Wherever.

Jimmy What can you do? You tell people, you warn 'em, you offer them a cordon bleu fucking menu, laid out tablecloth, six knives, forks and spoons and they still run off for a quick McDonalds up an alley. I don't know why I bother.

Shirley They'll be back soon. And it still leaves us, Jimmy.

Jimmy Too bloody true. And I'm having one of me visions, Shirl. (*Picks up an umbrella.*) Come on, then, cue action. Let's get rolling!

Panic for **Emma** *and* **Tony** *as* **Jimmy** *holds it as a camera.*

Jimmy Got everything, this place. Dream location. Costumes. Fantastic fucking cast, I could make a classic here. Can see it, yes, yes, modern remake – here you go, virginal nun gets fucked by missionary in the jungle and says, God bless you, kind sir. What film is that?

Emma 'Fraid you've got me there.

Jimmy Starring our very own and golden Audrey Hepburn. In – (*Waves at* **Shirley**.) *The Blue Nun's Story!*

A moment's stunned silence.

Jimmy You know it?

Emma I wouldn't quite have guessed it from your short précis.

Shirley Sounds fine to me, Jimmy.

Jimmy   Bless you, sweetheart. Never let me down yet. On your knees. (*As she kneels.*) To the manner born. OK, Tony, tek her whilst she's at prayer.

Tony   Pardon?

Jimmy   Up to you, son, to bring the poor lost gal into life.

Tony   Sorry . . . can we just pull back a second here . . . I can't make a film.

Jimmy   It's not a real fucking camera, you know. It's an umbrella. It's just a game to get us going.

Emma (*taking the umbrella*)   Don't open it indoors. Bad luck.

Tony   Well, yes, no, I appreciate that but . . . the part's not really me, is it? We should probably wait for Jack to come back – he's more the missionary. He can draw on his own . . .

Emma   Emotional recall.

Tony   Exactly, you see, I'd be miscast. I'm a doctor.

Shirley   Wasn't Peter Finch a doctor in the film?

Tony   What?

He turns to **Emma**.

Emma   Afraid so.

Shirley   Like Albert Schweitzer.

Jimmy   Perfect. Sex-starved Albert in the burning jungle. All he did all day was play with his organ.

Emma   That's not strictly accurate. He did amazing work with the lepers.

Jimmy   Yeh, well, we're skipping that bit.

Tony   No, no, sorry, I'm not playing Albert Schweitzer. Or Peter Finch. I can't do this. I just can't do it in front of other people, especially not you, her husband. I thought I might but . . .

Jimmy   What if I hide behind the bushes? I won't ask you to wave to me or anything.

Tony   I really can't.

Jimmy   Calm down. I'm a fellow man. I'm not without understanding. Been this route myself. I know women think we're all rampant beasts and one snap of a suspender belt and we're swinging through the trees with a lob on – but it's not like that, is it? We men have feelings. Some might go so far as to say we have hormones too. I understand your problem, can't just turn the tap on willy-nilly. You need some non-pressure stimulation. Bit of action elsewhere to get you going. That's fine. No problem.

Tony   Thank you for being so understanding.

Jimmy   Sensitivity's me middle name. OK, Emma.

She stares at him.

Emma   Sorry?

Jimmy   Come on, I'm just going to give you a seeing-to, to help get your husband juiced up.

Emma   Er . . .

Jimmy   It'll work, Tone, I guarantee it. Seeing a bloke rogering your missis. You'll be able to run a flag up the pole within five minutes.

Emma, *speechless, turns to* **Tony**.

Tony   Jimmy, God that is so kind, really, I'm moved but . . . you see, I've seen her, I've seen her with another fellow, yes, in the back of a car, wasn't it, Emma –

Emma   Yes, yes, completely forgot.

Tony   And bizarrely, it didn't work for me, not like it has for you. Opposite. Put me off completely. Must just have

different hormones from you. Really the last thing I want to
see.

Jimmy   So what's the problem? Don't tell me you don't
fancy my Shirl?

Tony   It's not that I don't fancy –

Jimmy   Bloody well hope not. I don't take that kind of
insult from any man.

Shirley   So you do?

Tony   Yes, of course, very much, but . . . not in public.
Private. Throw the keys on the table, that old stuff, you
know that would be absolutely but I know with you and
your husband your code . . . I understand, respect, respect,
yes respect that so . . . (*To* **Emma**.) Will you put that
fucking camera down! Umbrella. Shit. I'm getting . . . sorry,
it's just I'm afraid I thought I could but I couldn't in front of
– I'm not there in my life at that point and I'm just not
ready and . . . It's a terrible shame really but . . . Sorry.
Wish I . . . But . . . (*To* **Shirley**.) I'd love to have . . . with
you . . . Just . . .

Shirley   I understand.

Jimmy   What do you understand? He's ruining the whole
fucking film.

Tony   We're not making a fucking film!

Jimmy   We are, we are, we are in my mind, we are in
here where that fucking scoutmaster's hanging about and
I'm going to winkle the bastard out . . . And nobody's going
to compromise me – this is my life, you understand – I am
the director! This is the director's cut! And I'm making the
full fucking Fucking Blue Nun's fucking Story, so start
praying, Shirl, and Tony, take her, take her in prayer now!
Action!

Tony   You don't get it, do you? (*To* **Shirley**.) You understand, don't you? 'Scuse me, have to go to the bathroom.

He leaves.

Jimmy (*turning on* **Emma**)   What is wrong with that bloke of yours? I offer him the starring role and he goes all prima donna on me. Who the fuck does he think he is? It's a religious epic, for Christ's sake! Cliff Richard would have unzipped to play a part like this.

Emma   I think he's a bit shy.

Jimmy   A bit shy? A bit fucking shy? The man's at a swingers' party! It's like a bloke going on a real ale piss-up and ordering half a shandy – it dun't make no fucking sense.

Shirley   Let me have a word with him. Don't worry. It'll be all right.

Emma   I doubt you'll make him come round.

Shirley   Live in hope, eh?

She exits.

Jimmy   Why the fuck do I bother, can you tell me? I try to bring a little beauty into people's otherwise borin' grey lives and what thanks do you get? They spit in your face, don't even have the common courtesy to fuck your wife. I tell you if I was a real Eastern potent potentthingy offering the cream of me harem, the jewel in me crown, to some stuck-up little English officer and he turned me down, I'd chop his fucking head off, I'd feed his *cojones* to the crocodiles. I mean, your little stud has fucked everything by not fucking everything – what the fuck's that? And it means we can't fuck, for example, I know you'd set your heart on it but I can't do it wi'out Shirl here, this equality cuts both ways nowadays, much as you might be tempted. Matter of love and honour.

Emma (*nods*)   I'm obviously really disappointed but . . .

She sits down where she can occasionally whisper to **Paul**. *She's smiling.*

Jimmy   I know. Best not dwell on it. Can't tell, she might bring him round. Never let me down yet. (*Sighs; gazes around.*) We've got a conservatory, not like this, not filled with jungle plants, just a scattering of old crocks. Retirement home. We do everything we can for them you understand. Water, feed and weed. In summer we turn their wheelchairs round three times a day so they bake even. Christmas I sing 'em George Formby and Shirley gives 'em her 'Sally, Sally, pride of our alley'. Fancy finding pride in a bleedin' alley. I admire that. They're grand folk, actually, but you do sometimes feel you're just handling death warmed up. Nice to get out to somewhere where you press skin and it bounces back up.

Emma (*listening to* **Paul**)   No? (*Giggles.*) Really?

Jimmy *sits with a can of lager.*

Jimmy   Golden opportunity this. Should have brought me camera.

Emma (*to* **Paul**)   You're really into it, aren't you?

Jimmy   Dream on shooting a real movie, one with a proper story. I'm on an evening's course – film appreciation. Dead good, real hot debates on things like POV, point of view. You heard of that?

Emma   It rings a bell.

Jimmy   All about where's the camera? Where's the audience in relationship to what the camera shows? How do they relate, identify with the camera's position? Fucking amazing question in terms of porno you know. Take *Mary Poppins*, for example.

Emma   *Mary Poppins* is a porno?

Jimmy   No, no. (*Pauses.*) But it could be. No. Just an example they used – like, the chimney sweeps' number, where's the POV, whose eyes are the audience seeing it

through – is it with the kids going what the fuck, with Dick
van thingy and his sooty mates, smart-arsed seen-it-all Mary
Poppins herself, or is it the 'omniscient' i.e. God position?
See all, hear all, look down on the whole human race, we
the audience know everything when them in it know fuck-
all. POV affects us different. Do we identify, 'empathise',
bloody brilliant word that one, or sit in judgement and feel
fucking superior? So you ask yourself, what's the camera's
position, what's it to me, to me the audience? Is it constant?
Does it change? Does the audience change because of what
and how it sees? Ah. Then you get on to questions of
revelations. Is this moment a revelation for the character or
for the audience? Or both? And then smack in the middle of
supercalifragicunnilictus I had this brilliant idea, funny,
Edward reminded me of this, of mekin' a film of *Lady
Chatterley's Lover*.

Emma   Haven't there been half a dozen versions already?

Jimmy (*enacting this and coming close to hidden cameras*)   All
fucked, even the hard cores ones, cos they're not clear
what's the basic POV. It's dead obvious, really. It's her
husband's, Clifford, Lord Chatterley. Here's this war hero
who's had his balls blown off for king and country, and he's
got this bloody gorgeous steamy young wife and he knows
she's got needs, much as she's trying to deny them, like, for
his sake, and he's a good man, and in so many words he
gives her his blessing, go fuck my love, and then he's stuck at
home sweating out his fears and fantasies – and we see them
like dream nightmare sequences, 'orrible, 'til he can't take it
no more and he hits the woods. First 'omniscient' tracking
shot on Clifford belting his wheelchair through the trees.
Lots of dapple, no expense spared, dappled trees, dappled
horses, ducks and then he comes to the edge of a clearing
and the camera is suddenly for the first time directly from
his POV, what he sees, as he pulls aside these dappled leaves
like the lace curtain of a theatre and we pull focus from close
to distant and there's his missis platting daisy chains round
the gamekeeper's cock and getting it nice and ready and at
first we – him – 'empathy' – don't know if she knows he's

there but then she's riding him, hair swishing to and fro, sweat in river 'twixt her tits, and as she comes, her back arching, head, you know, she slowly looks towards the camera, him, us, and smiles. And we know she knows and were doing it for him as well.

Emma   And that's the climax?

Jimmy   Pull it off and it's simultaneous orgasm for characters and audience.

Emma   And what would that achieve?

Jimmy   Apart from coming together? First experience for a lot of folk is that anyway. But think POV. Her smile. What it would do is make the viewer feel that watching were OK. That they weren't just some dirty little voyeur invading people's private space. They were part of it. And maybe they could toss off for once without a feeling of . . . shame.

Emma   Do you feel shame?

Jimmy   Don't be daft, me, no, I'm talking about old blokes like.

Emma   And do you show your old blokes the films you've made?

Jimmy   You bonkers? Social services'd close us down in five minutes. I'd be a bloody pratt to put a poster up 'Saturday Night at the Movies'. Tonight – 'In a Spin'.

Emma (*smiles*)   Yes, it is.

Jimmy   What is?

Emma   The noise.

Jimmy (*confused*)   I can't hear nought.

A somewhat subdued **Edward** *and* **Jill** *appear through separate doors. The distant sound of a spin-dryer.*

Jimmy   Eh, school's out for summer. Did the headmaster put you straight, darling?

Jill   Yes, thank you.

Edward (*standing in the doorway*)   Where's my wife?

Emma   Sounds like she's doing some washing.

Edward   What?

Jimmy   Yeh, I can hear it now.

Edward   What?

Jimmy   Spin-dryer.

The rising sound of the spin-dryer reaching the climax of its cycle.

Jimmy   Bleddy 'ell. Your wife keeps nicking my best ideas, Eddie. My lawyer will be on the phone first thing.

Emma   There's no copyright on ideas.

Jimmy   How do you know?

Emma   Be flattered. This is life imitating art. No finer compliment.

Jimmy   Sounds like it's coming to the climax of its cycle.

Edward   What?

A sudden high female scream. Silence as the sound of the motor comes to a somewhat shuddering halt.

Jimmy   Should have been there. Bugger me.

Emma *nods and grins.* **Jill** *and* **Edward** *stand traumatised in the doorways looking back into the lounge. They slowly back into the conservatory as, first, a somewhat dishabille vicar, dog-collar turned heavenward, leans in* ADAM*'s door. And a rather shaky French tart appears in the other. Eventually . . .*

Jack   Are you sure you don't want the second rinse?

Jeni (*eventually*)   Later perhaps. (*Smiles, breathless.*) Bless you.

Jack   Bless you.

Fade lights to turn them into silhouettes with the tree between them.

Act Two

The Conservatory.

As before. Silence. The light moves back from silhouette to main state.

Jack   Are you sure you don't want the second rinse?

Jeni (*eventually*)   Later perhaps. (*Smiles, breathless.*) Bless you.

Jack   Bless you.

Silence.

Jack (*eventually*)   Is there a dishwasher?

Jeni   Yes.

Jack   Perhaps.

Jeni   Yes.

Edward   Why change when you've found a winner?

Jack   I was just concerned it might be a little too fast.

Jeni   Not at all.

Rather unsteadily she pours herself a strong drink.

Jack   Not entirely confident on how to control the speed.

Edward   Don't worry about it, Jack. I'm sure you were fantastic.

Jack   Well, thank you, I really appreciate that coming from her husband – that's really nice. Isn't it, Jill?

Jill   Yes.

Edward   So what did you discover amongst the dirty linen, *mon petit chou*?

Jeni   I've rather taken to this outfit, Edward. I think I might wear it for your inauguration.

Edward   It's in the Great Hall, not the Bois de Boulogne.

Jeni (*softly*)   Shame.

Emma   Inauguration?

Edward   That's exactly the word I was looking for.

Jeni   Inauguration?

Edward   Shame.

Jeni   Whoa, there, Edward. Isn't this exactly what I was supposed to do? Or is the truth that you never imagined me doing anything? You never imagined me at all? I was just here to give you a permit. Which I do freely. Wasn't the whole point that we were to share in this search together, face something, can't remember what, our fears, and perhaps even the discovery of our desires? Good, fine, going well, so how was your session with the salvation of the lower sixth? Don't we get a report? Letter to parents, end of term assessment? Come on, at least tell us how did she do in the orals?

Edward   Don't be obscene.

Jeni   Obscene? This is the fucking scene, Edward. God, I'm still shaking.

She pours herself another drink.

Edward   Foul-mouthed as well.

Jeni (*to* **Jack**)   Call a spade a spade, that's right, isn't it, Jimmy?

Jimmy   And a cock a cock.

Jeni   Thank you. Your husband has a beautiful cock, my dear.

Jill   Thank you.

Jeni   It has a most charming curve to the left.

Edward   Oh, whilst mine leans increasingly to the right, is that what you are inferring?

Jeni   I hadn't intended a political metaphor. Besides which, my long-term memory is not that good.

Edward   You fucking whore!

She throws her drink over him. **Edward** *looks almost ready to attack her.* **Jimmy** *quickly steps in between them.*

Jimmy   Hold on here, Edward, steady, steady. Come on, me old mate, listen to yourself, you're doing a classic bit of the old pot calling the kettle black here. Fair's fair, you've had your gander, you've got to let her be goosed an' all.

Jeni (*realising*)   Oh. (*Looks at* **Jill**.) But he hasn't, has he?

Jimmy   Hasn't what?

Edward   Don't you dare interrogate that innocent young girl.

Jeni   Has he?

Jill (*distressed, shakes her head*)   Is there something wrong with me?

Jeni (*gently*)   Don't take it personally, sweetheart. That was my mistake.

Edward   And what does that mean? So I'm to take all the blame, am I?

Jeni   Blame? Where are you, Edward?

Edward   I'm certainly not blaming her in any way.

Jack   Thank you.

Edward   It just didn't happen, that's all. It happens. Doesn't happen. Nothing unusual. It was a long drive . . . it might help if you took to the wheel occasionally, then all the preparing, clearing snow . . . Getting an Aga going can exhaust a battalion of the household cavalry. Perfectly understandable.

Jeni   Oh, Edward, I'm so sorry. You had such high hopes. Listen, love, don't blame yourself. It's not the end of the world, it really isn't.

Edward   Don't you dare to patronise me!

Jeni   What is it, Edward? What do you want to do, do you want to go back and start again from our certainties? There aren't any, Edward. You have to learn to accept.

Edward   Accept what? That my wife's a whore?

She shakes her head, and turns away, distressed.

Jack   I'm terribly sorry but I really feel you shouldn't talk to your wife like that.

Edward   Why don't you just fuck off and talk to your own wife before I –

Jimmy   Bloody hell, calm down everybody! Oil. Troubled waters. Please! None of this is that surprisin'. I mean, don't say I din't try to warn you – this going your own separate ways causes all manner of fuck-ups. Bloody 'ell, most of literature's about that, in't it? Best to get it out in the open, as the actress said to the vicar. So we can all have a butcher's and a goose and a gander, eh!

Edward   If you mention poultry just one more –

Jimmy   Don't start on me, mate, I'm trying to help you. I'm the one trying to work out how to raise your spirits from the dead. Not directly but (*Seeing* **Shirley** *and* **Tony** *return.*) Oh, thank God, here comes the Relief of bleedin' Mafeking.

*The nun (***Shirley***) and doctor (***Tony***) enter.*

Jimmy   In the nick of time. Everything all right, sweetheart? (**Shirley** *nods.*) That is a relief cos we're having a touch of the old 'One up one down one in a lady's chamber' fracas here. Now we've got to get all these good folk out on to the ballroom in quick step. So, come on, Shirl, you and Tony start us off with a little pas de deux. 'Come Dancing'. Come on, Shirl, let's show them. Take to the floor. A big hand for our stars for the evening – Tony and Shirl!

He holds out his arms to lead them both forth. They don't move. Silence.

Jimmy   What do you want? Music? Ravelli's fucking Bolero? Have I confused you? I'm using the word dance here as a metaphor for . . . I'm not with it. I thought? What's going on, Shirl?

Shirley   I'm sorry, Jimmy.

Jimmy   About what? (*Furious, to* **Tony**.) Don't say you're still refusing to fuck my wife?

Tony   Not at all. Quite the opposite. (*Pause.*) I already have.

Silence. **Tony** *has time to open a can of lager.*

Tony   Cheers.

Jimmy (*eventually*)   This is four kinds of ballocks, in't it, Shirl? Tell me.

Emma   Of course it is. It's a stupid game.

Jimmy   Course. Shirl'd never pull a trick like that on me, would you, petal?

Silence. **Shirley** *quietly gazes at her husband.*

Jimmy   Shirl? Shirl?

Shirley   It 'ad to happen some time, Jimmy.

Jimmy *groans.*

Shirley   I'm dead sorry, but . . .

As she reaches out to him, he's almost convulsed, fighting for breath.

Jimmy   Just fuck off!

Edward   I don't see your problem, Jimmy. Had your gander, now you have to let her be goosed.

Jimmy   Completely fuckin' different, this. Completely.

Shirley   It's hard, Jimmy. I know that.

Jimmy   Don't talk to me about fuckin' hard. You have no idea. You went with him without me to hold your hand? I can't credit it. No, Shirl, you can't put me through that hell again.

Jill   I don't quite understand. Why does it make such a difference if you're there or not?

Jimmy *can hardly speak.*

Shirley   He's scared, luv. Scared that without him to keep an eye on me I'll fall in love. Again.

Jeni   Again?

Shirley   Like what I did with Wally.

Jeni   But you didn't fall in love with Wally. You said you were just turned on by his wanting you.

Jill   Wally?

Edward   Some poor devil she picked up and then dumped.

Shirley   He dumped me.

Jeni   But you said –

Shirley   He dumped me.

Jimmy   No.

Shirley   Come on, Jimmy, you've always known that. You knew it even when I'd forgotten it meself.

Jimmy *stands in total shock.*

Shirley   After Wally, I won't going to be hurt by nobody. No way. Nobody were going to get near me. Sex were going to be like a nice cup of tea. Sometimes with an occasional cream éclair for a treat.

Jeni   Do you still love this Wally?

Shirley *looks at* **Jeni** *but doesn't reply.*

Jimmy   Why . . . with 'im? Why now?

Shirley   It were just the daftness of it all, Jimmy. I've
never had to try to persuade a bloke before, it's all been
fixed, we know what we'd all ordered. And then here I am
dressed as a mother superior gi'ing a bloke the hard sell to
persuade him to fuck me for you, and suddenly it were like I
were a kid back at school, one of them crazy teen times
where you spend ages standing in the pouring rain trying to
persuade some lad to go out with your best friend. (*Pause.*)
You are my best friend, Jimmy.

Jimmy   I'm not. Never want to be.

Shirley   So there you are, outside the school gates, or
dripping under a clump of dying trees, or who knows some
bowling alley bike shed bus shelter rabbiting on and . . . you
don't even ask yourself do yo' fancy him for yourself. What
does little miss piggie in the middle really want.

Jeni   And so you asked yourself?

Shirley   I did, yeh.

Jimmy   And what were the answer?

Shirley (*softly*)   You see, Jimmy, this is part of it, the truth
is . . . it's none of your business.

Jimmy   None of my business?

Shirley   No. It's private. That's the point.

Jimmy   What you doing? Private? I'm your husband.
You can't do this to me. Not again, Shirl, I'm not going to
take this lying down. Standing up, were the two of you
standing or . . . Were it the bathroom? Facing the mirror?
Or did you turn . . . did you kneel . . .Oh, shit. I'm not
taking it. I'll fight back this time. I'm from Hull. I'm from
Viking stock.

Shirley (*softly*)   His mother worked the docks.

Jimmy   Don't you dare say a word against her. We Vikings are a proud race. Bloody hell, we raped and pillaged all over the shop. So let's see how you like it. Have a taste of your own fucking medicine. (To **Jeni**.) Come on, you.

Jeni   Oh, not right now, thank you. It's my tea break.

She replenishes her glass.

Jimmy   Who then?

Emma *turns away.*

Jimmy   What about yo', luv?

Jill   I'm not sure.

Jimmy   Come on, one swallow don't make a summer.

Jill (*turning to* **Jack**)   I didn't . . .

Jack   It doesn't matter.

Jimmy   He says that. Let's put 'em to the test. Come on, kid, you and me are going outside to melt the snow with our lust.

Shirley   Jimmy, that's just plain stupid.

Jimmy   No it's not. Two can play at this fucking game.

Shirley   I meant going outside.

Jimmy   Don't pretend you care.

Shirley   I do care. At least put your coat on. And take an umbrella.

She tries to open the camera / umbrella.

Emma   Don't open it inside! Bad luck.

Shirley   Here.

Shirley *offers it to* **Jimmy**. *He refuses it.*

Jimmy   Stuff it. You're not my mother.

Shirley (*a beat*)   Exactly, Jimmy.

Jimmy   Oh, fuck you!

He grabs **Jill***'s hand and drags her out.* **Jack** *waves goodbye. Silence.*

Shirley   He's such a fool.

Tony   I'm sorry.

Shirley   Actually, Tony, strange as it sounds, this doesn't have a lot to do with you either. (*Sits down; stares at her hand.*) I'm still shaking. (*To herself.*) Why's that?

Jeni (*concerned*)   Jack? Shouldn't you be with her?

Jack (*a beat*)   No.

Shirley   They'll be back in five minutes. He fancies himself as Doctor Livingstone every time he goes in the back garden. Until it rains. Don't worry about them.

Jack   I'm not. (*Pause.*) Can I ask you a question?

Shirley *looks up at him.*

Jack   You wouldn't fancy . . .

Shirley   Not right now, precious.

Jack   You don't mind my asking, do you, only it's strange but I'm rather getting into this.

Shirley   Not at all. Bless you, Father.

Jack *looks at* **Emma**.

Emma   You've got be joking.

Jack   Yes. Probably.

He looks towards **Jeni** *who is keeping an eye on the sulking* **Edward**. **Jack** *helps himself to the vol-au-vents.* **Tony** *joins* **Emma** *downstage.*

Emma (*whispering*)   What the hell are you and Shirl playing at?

Tony   How can I put this elegantly – we were fucking in the bathroom.

Emma   Very funny.

Tony   It was certainly entertaining. Does it bother you?

Emma   It would do if I didn't know the truth.

Tony   Ah. Paul. You asked Paul? Yes, should have thought of that. Rather gives the game away, doesn't it? So what did Paul tell you?

Emma   That you two were just talking. Content unknown. But I guess about this number she wanted to pull on her husband.

Tony   Just talking? No mention of her crying out, then? Strange, it must have woken them up in Windermere. You must have heard it in here.

Emma   That wasn't you.

Tony   Well, I'm not taking all the credit, but to be honest I think I gave her my best shot. And I gave Paul his, too. The camera angled perfectly over the basin. Top quality in-built spotlights all around. Hardly a dark shadow anywhere. Paul's dream. I just don't understand why he would lie to you.

Emma   Is this some kind of game?

Tony   Yes.

Emma   Then let me in on it.

Tony   I'm trying to. Go spend a penny, Emma. Run back the tape in there. Let me know as a professional improviser what you think of my performance. I fucked her. I fucked her because for whatever reason she wanted it. And so did I. I fucked her for myself, I fucked her for Paul. And I fucked her – for you.

Emma   For me.

Tony   A little present. (*Pause as the truth sinks in.*) Oh, don't tell me you don't like it. I can hardly take it back.

Emma   Of course I don't like it.

Tony   Why not?

Emma   Because you're my fucking husband!

Jeni (*turning towards them*)   He's what?

Emma   Nothing. Nothing.

Tony   I'm her fucking husband. She's my fucking wife.

Emma   How could you fuck her?

Jeni   You said you weren't related. You only met up for sex.

Tony   The truth is exactly the opposite. We're married and don't meet for sex at all.

Edward   What's going on?

Tony   Should we tell them, Emma? Should we take a rare leap in the dark and give the old naked truth a bit of an outing? Try another new experience.

Emma   What is it you're playing at?

Tony   What are *you* playing at, Emma? That's the real question.

Shirley   Some problem?

Tony   Oh, how can I break this to you gently? Let's see. Emma and me, we work for a very talented, indeed charismatic leader, a visionary, wouldn't you say that, Emma? He's called Paul. We're supposed to be partners. It's not really true. No, no, it is true in one very particular sense. Emma here is his sexual partner.

Emma   Oh, God.

Tony It's a secret. I'm not supposed to know. A private contract. The details worked out in hotels, offices, telephone boxes old-style, the backs of cars. He's got an old classic Bentley. White leather seats. Beautiful. Irresistible. Isn't it, Emma?

Emma (*whispering into mike*) Paul! Stop this now. Tony, we need to talk about this. In private.

Tony Bathroom's free. Emma's about to dump me. We have one bit of dirty work to do together first, where my limited skills are still essential. I'm not exactly clear when I am to be informed of my redundancy – was that one of the things that came up during your intercourse with our master?

Emma It's not like that, Tony.

Tony What exactly is it like, Emma? I'm curious. Is the secrecy the kick? Does deception add a certain frisson? That special lingerie – the thongs of praise you fold up so carefully in tissue and hide away, at what point in the evening do you change back into the Marks and Sparks? Is it there whilst he's watching you or, like Superman, do you pop into the telephone box old-style on your way home? Does it add to the fun that the perfume you spray between your thighs is my traditional, unimaginative Christmas present? At least it's going to a good home. I see everything that's happening, can't help it, see every position, every arching of the sweating spine, but what I can't work out is how it feels? Am I there in your thoughts, is that part of it, are you fucking me in another sense, for what? Or, worse, am I nowhere, are you so caught up in the passion that I am simply erased? I'd love to know. (*Smiles.*) I'd really love to know where the fuck I am.

Silence.

Emma I think we should leave now.

Tony What? And ruin the show? A little unprofessional, darling.

Jack   What show?

Shirley   Is that why you fucked me, Tony? Just to get back at her.

Tony   Not planned, Shirl. But . . . It seemed like a good idea at the time. But then I forgot her. Emma, for a moment there, I erased you. It was a joy.

Emma   Oh, Tony, believe me, I didn't do it to hurt you.

Edward   Everyone always says that about betrayal.

Jack   What if she's telling the truth?

Tony   You think I should forgive her, Vicar?

Jack   Well, I don't . . . perhaps there's nothing ultimately to forgive. Maybe love just changes. After all, it's not fixed in aspic. We're human. We don't really control love, do we? It's more like a river we're swept away in. To be honest, I've often thought God was a little hard on Adam and Eve. He thought they'd betrayed him. I'm not convinced that was what they intended. Or indeed that ultimately they had much choice.

Edward   Another few hours in that collar and you'll be baptising babies.

Jeni   You're a good man, Jack.

Jack   I'm not supposed to be, that's my problem.

Edward   I've had enough of all this naked truth for one night.

Tony   Oh, sorry, no, one second, excuse me, I've forgotten the most important bit.

Edward   If it's more about betrayal?

Tony   Well, it is actually, but of a somewhat different kind.

Jeni   Shouldn't this be private, just between the two of you?

Tony   That's rather against the spirit of the occasion, isn't it? Besides, I'm afraid this rather involves all of you.

Emma   No, Tony. Please, don't.

Tony   Touching a nerve now?

Emma (*into the mike*)   Stop this, stop this now!

Tony   She's not talking to me, by the way.

Jack   Who's she talking to, God?

Tony   Damn close.

Emma   Stop it! (*To* **Tony**.) Please, Tony, stop it.

Tony   You know what men are like, once started. You see what we've omitted to mention to you was that we –

A figure almost crashes against **Adam**'s *door.*

Edward   Oh, Christ!

A naked **Jimmy** *almost encased in white and snow staggers in.* **Emma** *stares transfixed as he falls into her arms.*

Shirley (*panicking*)   Oh, Jimmy! Jimmy, you stupid bugger!

Emma   He's dead!

Shirley   Oh, my God, no!

She claws him away from **Emma**, *as a shaking* **Jill**, *shimmering in ice, enters through* **EVE**'s *door.*

Jill   I couldn't stop him. He stripped off his clothes, started jumping up and down beating himself with twigs, screaming it was some Viking ritual, then . . . the ice broke on the pond –

Shirley   Help him, somebody help him!

Jeni   Tony!

Tony   What?

Jeni   You're a doctor.

Tony   I'm not a real doctor.

Jeni   Oh, no, right, shit.

Shirley   Get us a real one!

Jack   Let me try.

Edward   What do you know?

Jack   I learned basics in Africa.

Jill   I'm sorry. I've killed your husband. I'm wicked. Someone needs to stop me.

Shirley   Excuse me, you're not tekin' the credit. If anyone killed him, it were me, his wife.

Edward   Why don't you both shake hands and admit you're all the whole lot of you as bad as each other?

Jeni   What's this, Edward, not the old curse of Eve? I'm not having that.

Jack (*to* **Tony**)   Help me get him on the lounger.

Edward   Butter wouldn't melt on your bum would it, little miss perfect.

Tony   God, he's a dead weight.

Jeni   It was you who wanted to be Marlon Brando. I was worried about the carpet.

Edward   I'm talking about how you've corrupted this innocent young lad here.

Jill   You've got to save him, Jack!

Jeni   Let me tell you something, Witchfinder fucking General. I've felt guilty for twenty years when I'd done nothing, and now I've done something that you think I should be feeling guilty about, I don't, not at all.

Shirley   What's the matter with him?

Edward   That's because like the rest of your women's tribe you've gone too far to be able to tell the difference.

Jack   Could be anything – heart attack, hypothermia, give me the stethoscope.

Jeni   Oh, go butter your own buns and stuff your vol-au-vents.

Shirley *rips it off* **Tony***'s head. He cries out.*

Shirley   Sorry.

Edward   You can't deny my basic argument.

Tony   You nearly ripped my ears off!

Emma   It's you men who started it all. The whole history of the patriarchy clearly –

Edward   Jack, did you start all this?

Jack   What's wrong with the stethoscope?

Shirley   It in't real. We can't afford real props!

Jack (*throwing it away*)   Hell!

Edward   Course he didn't. No more than Adam over there. He was happy skipping around dreaming up names for the flora and fauna. Till the snake rises up. And who is it the snake talked to first?

Shirley   Is he breathing?

Emma   You're not going to make out the snake isn't the penis, are you ?

Jack   Sorry, don't mean to interrupt but there isn't actually a penis in the story. Literally speaking. There's an apple.

Shirley   What the fuck are you doing? There's a man dying here!

Jack   Oh, yeh, sorry. Phone for an ambulance, someone.

Tony   Emma! Tell Paul!

Edward   I don't deny the snake is the penis. But who starts playing with it first, eh? Answer me that.

Shirley   He's freezing to death.

Edward   Exactly.

Jill   Warm him with your body.

Jack *lies on him.*

Emma   I'm sorry, I may not be as white as the driven snow, but I'm not standing here and letting women take all the blame just because for once they've decided to stand up and fight for their own desires –

Tony   Is that what you were doing? It was a fight, was it? It feels more like a mugging in the dark.

Jack   I'm freezing myself.

Shirley   At least you're alive.

Edward   You're just scared to face up to your true nature.

Shirley   Give him the last rites.

Jeni   Curving to the right again, Edward.

Jill   I'm not a Catholic.

Edward   Leave my penis out of this.

Shirley   Neither's he.

Jeni   That's not difficult, is it?

Jack   There's no time for a last-minute conversion. Pray, pray if you want to, just get out of the way!

Shirley *kneels in prayer.*

Tony   Is the ambulance on its way?

Edward   We must stop confusing metaphors with reality.

Jill   Give him the kiss of life.

Jack *does so.*

Emma   Paul! Paul! Get an ambulance.

Jeni   Oh, Edward, where the hell are we . . . ?

Shirley   Saint Paul's no good. Pray to Saint Christopher. Or Mary, the Virgin Mary.

Emma (*desperately*)   Why isn't he answering me?

Tony   He's loving every second of it. (*Leans over her.*) You bastard!

Jeni   Leave her be.

Jack *starts to thump* **Jimmy**'s *heart.*

Emma   Where's a phone? Anybody got a phone?

Jeni (*picks up a planted mobile phone / camera*)   Here.

Emma   That's not a phone.

Jeni   Well, what on earth is it?

Tony   Good question is that.

Jack   Hold on! Hold everything. He's alive.

Shirley   How can you tell?

He slowly slides off **Jimmy**. *They stare at his groin.*

Jeni   Goodness.

Jill   It's a miracle.

Shirley   You can say that again.

Jill   Thank you, Jesus.

Silence.

Jack   Wrap him in something warm.

Shirley *takes off her nun's habit.*

Emma   Do we still need the ambulance?

Jack   Hold on. It might just have been a panic attack. If it is, the recovery rate will be very fast. If not, they'd probably be too . . . Let's just get him thawed out and see.

They put him in the habit.

Jill   He's coming round.

Jimmy (*almost inaudible*)   Am I in heaven?

Shirley   By the looks of it, kid.

Jimmy   Stone me. Oh . . . (*Mumbles.*) Boy Scouts . . .

He fades away again.

Shirley   He's fading, he's fading. Talk him back.

Jack   Jimmy, can you hear me? Come on, Jimmy, come back to us. You like it here. You've still got things to do here, there's folk who love you.

Edward   Don't push it too far.

Jack   You haven't given of your best yet. Turn back from the light, see us down here in the dark of the jungle. We want you. We need you. Come back, Jimmy. Come back. There'll be another time. Come back and talk to us, share with us.

Jimmy *slowly stirs into life.*

Jimmy   'All things bright and beautiful . . .'

Shirley   You all right, petal?

Jimmy (*smiling*)   Oh, God, I don't half feel queer. I were, I've been . . . how long were I dead?

Shirley   A few minutes.

Jack   You weren't actually –

Jimmy   I were in heaven. Bloody hell, fancy that. Fancy it really existing.

Edward   Fancy they let you in.

Jimmy   Yeh. (*Pause.*) Fancy. (*Smiles.*)

Jill   You actually went to heaven?

Jimmy   Absolutely.

Edward   Did they serve lager?

Jeni   Shut up.

Jill   Go on, what was it like?

Jimmy   Oh, tricky that. Well, there were what you expect, prayers and the angels and all that . . . and the Garden, mowed, neat herbaceous borders and there were apple trees, you could see the dew on the leaves, like diamond earrings on a duchess . . . and . . . oh yeh, there were a bloody huge snake (*Smiles.*) but it was dead nice and friendly, I've never stroked a snake before and it were grand. (*Sighs, smiles.*) Bugger me, you can never tell what's through the next door, can you? One minute I'm hopping up and down on the ice with frostbite in my *cajones*, the next I'm there, lying on me back on a bank of golden daffs. And that was just the start of it. I coun't move. I could feel the weight of my body but I couldn't shift nought and then there was a shadow against the sun, and next thing I know is Jesus was there, Jesus comes to me, and he holds me in his arms and he kisses me and he hold me like a bride, like I were the bride of Christ, and then . . .

Shirley   Yes?

Jimmy   And then . . . then he resurrected me, and do you know what the first blessed sign was . . .

Edward   An erection.

Jimmy   Have you been there yourself?

Jeni   Not recently.

Jimmy   Unbelievable.

Edward   Exactly.

Jimmy (*shaking himself out of his reverie*)   I'd have stayed there but the Lord wanted me to come back. To tell you the truth.

Edward   Which is?

Jimmy (*slowly*)   What we're doing here, it in't wrong. No shame. No blame. We're searching for . . . What did you call it?

Jack   Agape?

Jimmy   Aye. Agape. (*Decisively.*) That's what I've come back to tell the world. Agape Rules OK.

Edward   Oh, spare me.

Jimmy   What we are doing is holy. The truth should be exposed to the light.

Edward   You want the truth, O Lord? Well let me oblige you.

Jeni   No.

Edward   The truth is you went outside to play Viking ball-games, got frostbite in your nether regions, and when you can't get it up with this young girl, you go hopping mad, turn into the Iceman cometh, and get brought round by Jack the vicar here who gives you the kiss of life that in turn brings to the surface your latent homosexuality that you have been sublimating by watching your wife with the cocks you secretly fancy, and you have now glossed all that up into some deep and meaningful religious experience. It's crap.

Jimmy *for once is reduced to silence. He stares around.*

Jeni   Cruel.

Edward   Is it truth time or not?

Jeni   Only if you've the guts to face your own.

Jimmy *stares at* **Shirley** *and then at* **Tony**. *And back again to* **Jack** *who smiles at him.*

Shirley   Jimmy.

Jeni   Don't listen to him, Jimmy.

Jimmy (*eventually*)   No, no, hang on, he might be right.

Edward   Of course I'm right.

Jimmy   It's certainly an interpretation.

Edward   It's what happened.

Jimmy   Hold on, I can see that but . . . no, I'm not denying . . . it's possible. It's possible you both could be right.

Edward   Both?

Jimmy   You and Jesus. He who forgives us all our sins.

Jack   Perhaps, as you say, there's no sins to forgive.

Jimmy   Perhaps that's what he really came to tell us.

Jack   Perhaps.

Jimmy   Hallelujah.

Edward (*exhausted*)   I give up. We are clearly all certifiably insane and need locking away. O Lord, let your divine retribution fall upon our heads. Amen. That's it. Nothing else to do but to leave with our tails between our legs and die of exposure in the snow.

Edward *starts taking off his costume.*

Tony   You can die of exposure in the heat as well.

Edward   What does that cryptic remark mean?

Tony (*looking at* **Emma**)   There are many different kinds of exposures.

Emma   Tony, please.

Tony   For example, take this umbrella. Its exposure is set much higher than, say, this mobile phone. Or indeed that of the briefcase.

Edward   What on earth are you talking about?

Tony   Oh, sorry, not being very clear. (*As he reveals the cameras. In a Japanese accent.*) My fliend, this not bliefcase. This velly expensive Japanese camela. This not mobile phone but velly expensive Amelican spy camela. Velly good wide lens. Sound quality also velly, velly good. Velly good for catching nanny shaking the baby or shagging your husband.

Emma   Why are you determined to destroy everything we've —

Tony (*picking up umbrella*)   This English umblella, you guess, not umblella. Camela. Not velly expensive, but velly good for close-up. Smile please, Emma.

Jeni   Wait. You're making some kind of film?

Tony   Now you're getting the picture.

Edward   Well, I'm not. What's going on here?

Emma (*quietly*)   He's fucking his wife.

Jimmy   Thought it was my wife he fucked. What have I missed?

Tony   Don't panic, Jimmy, this is your dream orgy. Tonight everybody gets fucked.

Edward   What do you mean everyone?

Tony   The cameras are all over the house. Here, of course, and obviously the kitchen to capture the saga of the washday blues . . . (*Smiles at* **Jeni** *and* **Jack**.) . . . the headmaster's study, looking forward to seeing sex at St Trinians, Edward (**Edward** *horrified.*), and, of course, the bathroom for the Blue Nun's Story.

Shirley   You filmed us?

Jimmy   So I *will* get to see you.

Tony   You and a few others.

Shirley   The whole point was I didn't want that filmed.
Just for once, it was to be private.

Tony   Sorry.

Shirley   Sorry?

Jill   What do you mean – others? Who else is going to see
it?

Tony   I'm afraid it's not just a charming memento for me
and Emma. We're making a sensitive documentary here.
Well, perhaps sensitive is not quite the right word.
Sensational! Sorry, that's what I meant – a sensational
documentary. 'Swingtime'. Warts, willies and all.

Stunned silence.

Emma   You fool.

Tony   I can't argue with that.

Edward   Documentary?

Tony   Almost there. Take your time. We've plenty of
tape. (*Silence. He turns to smile at* **Emma**.) How's it going for
you, my love? It does take time for it all to sink in, doesn't
it? Personally I think this will be the most interesting section.
Much more than the bonking. Now at this moment
everybody is really stripped bare. Like one of those
nightmares where you find yourself running naked through
the streets and you desperately want to wake up and be free
of it. But you can't. Not this time. Because this is being
awake. Wow. Bit embarrassing. If only the ground would
open up and swallow me. It's quaking enough. Oh, no,
that's me. I'm doing the shaking.

*He stares at his hand, smiles, sits down and opens another can of lager.
Anyone else who is moving seems to be doing so in slow motion.*

Jill   Oh, no, I'm sorry, you can't. You can't do that. It
would mean I'd ruined everything if you . . . No. Jack, you
mustn't let them. Please.

Jack   Oh, yes, no, excuse me.

Tony   Yes.

Jack   I'm terribly sorry but I'm afraid you won't be able to show that.

Tony   Oh. Disappointment. Mind telling me why not?

Jack   It's rather personal.

Tony   Yes?

Jack   It's just it would harm a lot of people.

Tony   A little more, perhaps, to draw out my hidden compassion?

Jack   You see . . . (*Sighs.*) Well, we, Jill and I, we do a lot of work with disadvantaged children. It's a church-funded scheme, basically, although it's not in any way, you know, simply a . . . When I say disadvantaged, I mean . . . You can't imagine what some of these kids have been through. All kinds of . . . abuse and . . . Well, they're all over the . . . You see, if this became . . . well, the Church, I'm pretty certain they wouldn't really, not their kind of, I mean, that's the whole point why we are . . . Well, they'd stop us instantly. They would hardly consider an activity like this as seemly for a . . .

Tony   For who?

Jill   You have to tell him.

Jack (*pauses*)   For a vicar.

Tony   Amazing. A sheep in sheep's clothing. That's a very cunning disguise, Jack.

Jack   It's my first posting. Welwyn Garden City.

Jill   They'll expel us.

Tony   Expelled from Welwyn Garden? Some might consider that a blessing.

Jack   No. No, not just . . . No, they'll expel me from the Church.

Jeni   Thought you'd already left?

Jack   No.

Jill   We wanted to change it from within.

Jack   That's right. There's so much that's admirable in the teachings of Jesus, it's the Church that went up the wrong alley when it came to sex. That's nothing to do with Jesus. I mean (*To* **Jeni**.) he had friends who wore berets and stood on street corners under flaming torches and . . . Or the Jewish equivalent. No, it was Saint Paul who was really the problem.

Tony   Tell me.

Jimmy   So you do believe in God after all?

Jack   Well, no, not God, no, not exactly, no.

Jeni   Isn't that something of a problem for a vicar?

Jack   No. None of the clergy does. We just agreed to keep it a secret so as not to confuse people.

Jimmy   I'm confused.

Jill (*stunned*)   You don't believe in God? Why have you never mentioned this to me? Am I one of those people you didn't want to confuse?

Jack   I was going to tell you. Just never was the right time. And it didn't seem terribly important.

Jill   Not believing in Jesus?

Jack   I do believe in Jesus. Well, the human bit.

Jill   The human bit?

Jeni   Doesn't that rather diminish his significance?

Jack   Not to me, no. Quite the contrary.

Edward   Excuse me. Fascinating as this theological debate is, we seem to be somewhat straying off the point here.

Jeni   Which is?

Edward   This pair are about to crucify the lot of us.

Jill (*repeating*)   The human bit?

Shirley   Yes, but they won't name us, will you, I mean you won't show what we look like? There'll just be them wobbly blobs all over our faces?

Edward   No change there, then.

Jeni   Edward!

Tony   Hate to disappoint you once again, Shirl, but this one's the full monty.

Shirley   Oh, fuck.

Jimmy   Not the end of the world, is it?

Shirley   Social Services will close us down in five minutes.

Jimmy (*pauses*)   Oh, God.

Edward   You are going to destroy all of us.

Jack   Why would you do that?

Edward   You want to take everybody down with you just because your own life is in ruins.

Tony   Perfectly normal human reaction, don't you think?

Jack   No. I don't.

Edward   I could kill you. I really could.

Tony   Too late. I've committed suicide already.

He smiles at **Emma**.

Jill (*desperate*)   You can't do this. You really can't.

Edward   Damn right he can't. I'll have every lawyer in the country all over you. You'll never be allowed to transmit one single frame of this.

Tony   Hm.

Edward   There. Got you. You shouldn't have let the cat out of the bag so early.

Tony (*nods, a beat*)   Emma, would you like to tell them about the vision of Saint Paul on the road to . . . Where the hell was it?

Jack   Damascus.

Tony   Detroit. Some kind of congress. Wasn't it, Emma?

Jimmy   Who's Saint Paul?

Jill   The founder of the early –

Jeni   He's Emma's lover.

Jimmy   She's fucking a saint?

Tony   That's another interesting theological debate. Emma? She's awaiting his divine assent. (*Silence.*) So risk it, go it alone, Emma. No? (*Sighs.*) OK. Our producer Saint Paul is actually a lawyer. Specialises in censorship laws, and how to get round them. Which is why he's opening his new TV series on the Internet. The Revelations Exposé Channel, kicking the shit out of corrupt politicians, drug dealers, pimps, fascists . . . all the slime that lurks under the rocks upon which our noble society is built. That's where we come in – the Laurel and Hardy of undercover doc-makers. And he needed a hot sexy show to kick it off. Sexy being the key media word here to get the subscribers on board. And that's where you come in.

Edward   That's what you think. I swear to you this will never be transmitted.

Tony   You're missing the point, Edward.

Edward   What point?

Tony   Even as we speak and breath, Saint Paul is in his little studio van receiving and editing our images via the marvel of satellite by which he is also simultaneously transmitting them to a teeny little island in the sun where there's no censorship laws cos there's only one monkey living there and that said monkey has been trained to press the transmit button on to the Internet for the price of a banana. And right now he's probably finishing it off. So come on, guys and gals, smile and wave at the monkey, you're live on candid camera.

A frozen silence.

Tony (*eventually*)   You can move. It won't spoil the group photo.

Jack *and* **Jill** *vanish behind potted plants and Grecian urns,* **Edward** *dives for cover,* **Shirley** *grabs her fleece and slides off into the undergrowth.* **Jimmy**, *sitting on the lounger, simply disappears inside his habit. Only* **Jeni** *is left.* **Emma** *sits quietly watching* **Tony**. **Tony** *sits by* **Jimmy**.

Tony   You disappoint me, Jimmy, I thought you were into spreading the good news.

Jimmy (*voice*)   Didn't reckon on being a fuckin' martyr.

Tony   Not always a matter of choice.

Tony *pats him on the thigh.* **Edward** *hisses at* **Jeni**.

Edward   Get down, woman. Get down.

Jeni (*softly, distraught*)   The twins, Edward. What are they going to say? How are they going to feel? (*To* **Tony**.) Where's the cameras?

Tony   Everywhere.

Jeni (*nods; attempts to tidy herself up*)   I'm sorry, sweethearts. I didn't mean to embarrass you. Nothing worse than to be shamed by your own parents. But you're not responsible, darlings, it's not your fault the way your parents have turned out. Don't blame yourselves. You did your best.

Edward (*moving from behind one statue to another*)   Jeni, come on, shut up and get your head down.

Jeni   Do they have to hear you saying dirty things like that?

Edward   You're drunk, woman.

Jeni   The Tarot reading, Edward?

Edward   Tarot?

Jeni   Did you make it up?

Edward   What on earth are you –

Jeni   Doesn't matter. I have my own prophecy now to fulfil. Where's my knickers?

Edward (*head appearing*)   What?

Jeni   Ah, in my handbag (*As she digs them out: Lady Bracknell.*) A handbag? (*Giggles.*)

Edward (*appearing*)   What the hell are you doing?

Jeni   I dedicate this song to one lonely, hard-working and underpaid monkey. I hope you like it.

Jeni *places the knickers on her head. Then, singing and dancing.*
   Come Mister Tallyman, tally me bananas
   Daylight come and I want to go home
   Come Mister Tallyman, tally me bananas
   Daylight come and me wanna go home

She subsides.

Edward   Come on, Jeni, just calm down. I'll take you home.

He tries to cover his face as he moves towards her.

Jeni (*suddenly*)
   Day O, Day O, daylight comes
   And I want to go home.

(*Spoken.*) How does it go?

(*Sings*.) 'Hide the deadly black tarantula –'

(*Spoken*) Fuck the black tarantula I don't care –

(*Sings*)
  Six foot seven foot eight foot bunch
  Daylight comes and –

(*Spoken*.) Fucking furry spider. Sorry, kids. Really sorry.

She crumples and sits by the fountain. Heads begin to appear into view like gophers in the desert. **Edward** *stands over her. He stares around as though expecting some kind of help.* **Tony** *smiles at him and angles the 'briefcase' on him.*

Jimmy (*appearing*)   Switch them off. Switch all the cameras off!

Edward   No.

Tony   Over to you, Edward. 'Thought for the Day' today is from Mr Chips of Ecclestone College. It's entitled . . . ?

Edward (*eventually, quietly*)   Fuck you.

Tony   Catchy. I like it.

Edward   Fuck you! (*Pointing at the camera*.) And you. Fuck off, all of you! You and the whole fucking heavenly host out there. You gutless load of shits, you who hide behind your curtains, watching the flickering light in the corner with all the doors locked, and all you want to do is glory in other folks' shame, that's it, isn't it, you want the witch hunt, you want to be able to laugh at and mock, and wiggle your poxy little finger, you want to feel self-righteous same time as you play with yourselves. Fuck you, fuck you all. I'm not ashamed, I'm not goin' to accept your judgement, I couldn't get it up, did that give you a laugh, I don't give a fuck. Let me tell you, you shitbag angels, this woman, these people, these daft stupid fools, they have more guts in their little male or female pinkies that they might or might not get up once in a fucking blood moon than the whole cloud nine of you spineless shits put together. It's you, it's you who should

be shamed. It's you who are the sad fuckers. I may drool
and droop but at least I'm still fighting. I'm not dead. I'm
still on the front line. In thought, word and fucking deed.
And if this nun here wants a cock at both ends for
Christmas, or this young innocent schoolgirl desires more
than jolly hockey sticks, or even if she my wife, my noble
mad south by south-west demented wife, wants to sit on a
spin-dryer dressed up as a tart and fuck a man with a north
by north-west lilt to his cock, well, I can't believe I'm saying
this but who gives a fuck, what the fuck's that got to do wi'
you, she's every right, because she's had the guts to go into
the dark and in there there are panics, you, OK, you grab
on to anything in the dark, that's human and it doesn't
mean she's a tart, she's just someone looking and anyway
even if she was . . . she, looking back, I don't know, how can
I know, maybe it's nice to know as a woman you still have
the power to charm snakes and the snakes don't mind, I
don't know, I'm not a woman, they're a complete and utter
fucking mystery to me . . . A mystery. But a mystery to be
respected. Jesus Christ, she's human, that's all. Are you? Are
you? What the fuck do you think you are, Paul and all your
disciples? Angels in hell? Just fuck the fuck off. Fuck.

He's exhausted. **Jeni** *looks up at him.* **Shirley** *has risen up and
slowly applauds.*

Shirley   That was great. (*Nods.*) Thank you.

Edward (*shaking*)   Kind. Very kind. Basically it's the . . . I
. . . the thesis of my new book. *Pre-Raphaelites and Sexual
Transgression.* Not written exactly in quite those words of
course. Not in the demotic.

Jack (*voice*)   Perhaps it should be.

Jimmy (*head appearing*)   Yep. Gi' folk like me a chance to
understand it.

Edward   Perhaps.

Tony   It was certainly a terrific plug for your book. Should shift a few copies for you. Save the outfit for the launch, Jeni. Brilliant photo opportunity.

Jeni   Perhaps. (*Pause.*) Edward?

Edward *turns to her, then turns away.*

Edward (*quietly*)   Can we switch all the cameras off now?

Emma   No need. Paul stopped transmitting ages ago.

Jeni   So when did he end it? Was it before I . . . Before I made my apology?

Emma   Yes.

Jeni   Oh. (*Pause.*) Good.

Shirley   Shame they won't have heard Edward's speech though.

Edward   Well . . .

Jeni   No, that's true. It is.

Jack (*appearing*)   Jill. 'Come out, come out, wherever you are.'

Jill (*voice*)   I can't look at you.

Jack   I'm not that bad, am I?

She slowly rises up.

Jill   It's me. It's me.

He looks at her. She looks away.

Jimmy   So when exactly did this Saint Paul bloke stop it? Was it before my big number, eh?

Emma   As my husband launched into our domestic problems.

Jimmy   Now that is a shame. Would have liked a copy of that.

Jeni   Was it getting get too hot for your boyfriend?

Emma   It was of no interest to our viewers. They'd got what they came for.

Edward   Lucky them.

Tony   Oh, is that what Paul whispered in your ear? Show over? And you believed him? (*Smiling.*) He's handed a dream tale of sex, betrayal and divine retribution. A cast of tarts and vicars, doctors and nurses, teachers and schoolgirls and for the cherry on the cake, he's even got his own film-makers burning at the stake. Emma? No interest to our viewers? Really? That's like saying the Inquisition walked away before lighting the pyres. Or the Romans left before the lions came on.

Emma   I don't care about the Romans, I'm the one who's leaving, Tony.

Tony   Ask Paul.

Emma   He's not there. It's over.

As she turns to leave, he grabs hold of her and leans into her breast.

Tony   Paul, me old mate, you can't let her go, sunshine. Human interest. Come on, you've got a great ending here. Tell her now. Hit her with the truth. Why wait until it's off-screen and we can't all share in the pleasure.

Emma   You're just being stupid, Tony. He's not there, it's finished, he's –

She stops in her tracks. She is listening.

Tony   What's he saying, Emma? Is he telling you this is sexier than sex, sexier than even the back of a Bentley? This is what the audience love, what he loves, this is true love, watching beauty get really fucked. And knowing so many others are watching with you. 'You have to understand, my love. There's a greater purpose in this life than just us, just our own selfish happiness. There's ratings. Sometimes there must be sacrifice. Strike the match. Let the blaze begin. Reality TV – the Auto Da Fe. Burn baby burn.'

Everyone watches **Emma** *burn. No one moves.*

Tony   Close-up reaction shot of Emma. Fast intercuts of close-up shots of those watching. Different expressions, some uncertain, fascinated, sickened, joyful, whatever. Track in above the flames on Emma's face as the skin bubbles and the years of expensive moisturiser are laid to waste. To wide master of all assembled. No movement. Freeze as tableau. Fade colour into black and white. Creep up the planned credit music – Joni Mitchell's 'Woodstock' – 'We are stardust/we are golden/and we've got to get ourselves/back to the garden'. Sung unaccompanied, smoky, chanteuse female voice, the lyrics now weighted by heavy postmodern irony. Slow fade to grey grain to black over ten seconds. Nine. Eight. Seven. Six. Five. Four. Three. Two. One. And out.

Silence.

Tony   Thank you, everyone. That's a wrap. Well done.

No one moves. All seem emotionally dazed. **Emma** *unplugs her earpiece and lets it fall to the ground. She looks faint.* **Shirley** *gently touches her shoulder.* **Emma** *flinches, sits down with her briefcase on her knee, as though waiting for some midnight train.*

Tony   Post-shoot party. Bar's open.

Tony *gets himself a drink.*

Edward (*to* **Tony**)   That was truly cruel. (*Pauses.*) I would have done the same.

Edward *pours himself a drink. The others are like inhabitants in the ruins of a bomb raid.*

Jack (*to* **Emma**)   Would you like some water?

Emma *does not respond.*

Jack   So hot now.

Jill   We're all of us burning up, aren't we?

Jack   Jill.

Jill   What about the kids? What about Sandy and Bethany? We'll just help them clock up one more abuse to add to their list. They don't deserve that.

Jack   They won't understand any of this.

Jill   Our leaving them, Jack. I mean, our desertion.

Jack *stands in silence.*

Jeni (*approaches* **Edward**)   Do you so desperately want to be vice-chancellor?

Edward   I don't know what I want, Jeni. I wanted the girl. That's what I thought. I don't seem to have any real desire, just imagined that I did. Is that possible?

Jeni (*shrugs*)   Well, you said we were here to share our uncertainties, and search for the truth.

Edward   And what's the truth?

Jeni   That we are uncertain? That's what we are? Of course I can't be certain.

Edward   Could you desire me?

Jeni   I've so much dirty washing still to get through, Edward.

She takes the drink and turns to watch as **Tony** *approaches* **Emma** *with a tray of vol-au-vents.*

Emma   I didn't do it to hurt you.

Tony   I believe you. You didn't even give me a thought.

Emma   Oh, but I did.

Tony   Ballocks. Try a vol-au-vent. Who you crying for? Me? You? Or out of an overwhelming compassion for the world in general?

Emma   What more do you want, Tony? You've destroyed us both.

Tony   If only. No, darling, I've made you. The phone will be on meltdown with offers – late-night chat show hostess, the Scarlet Woman presents . . . no faster way to become the media star than getting your knickers in a twist in public. A blow-job in a lay-by. A lay in a Bentley. I should ask for a percentage.

Emma   You imagine that's what I'd want?

Tony   Don't ask me. I'm the last person to ask.

He moves off with the tray. Through the following **Jeni** *wanders over and sits by* **Emma**.

Jimmy   What we going to do wi' all them empty wheelchairs?

Shirley   They'll buy us out as a job lot. Lock, stock and residents.

Jimmy   But who's going to sing 'em 'Sally, pride of our alley'? (*Quietly.*) 'You're more than the whole world to me.'

Shirley   Don't, Jimmy.

Jimmy (*quietly*)   So what you going to do – go looking for Wally?

Shirley   No.

Jimmy   Or some other bloke who can hurt you?

Shirley   Not hurt me, Jimmy. That's not it.

Tony   Vol-au-vent?

Shirley   I haven't forgiven you. (*Taking one.*) Thank you.

Tony *offers* **Jimmy** *one*.

Jimmy (*pauses*)   Ta.

Jill   What have I done? I've even made you lose your faith.

Jack   Actually I never really had any.

Shirley   Delicious.

Jill   What do you mean?

Jeni   My mother's recipe.

Jack   I saw you on freshers' day. I followed you. I'd have signed up for any club that took your fancy. I was just praying it wasn't mountain climbing. Or potholing. Potholing would have been hell.

Shirley   You must let me have it.

Jill   So I corrupted you from the very beginning?

Jeni   It's a family secret.

Jill   Oh, what can I say? Edward's right about what he said, we women, we corrupt without even having to think about it. Just by the look of us. The smell.

Jack   No.

Jill   Come on, look at me tonight, I've driven one man half crazy, nearly killed another, and drove a third, my husband, to a spin-dryer and prostitutes. And I haven't even had a fuck myself yet! Not even got started. No, Edward . . . Like my father, my father was right. He was right all the time. I tried to deny it, to forget it, but . . .

Jack (*quietly*)   At last. I've been waiting for years to talk about him. Listen, my love, your father, he was a real fucker. (*With real venom.*) A real fucker!

She stares up at him.

Jack   It wasn't you.

Jill (*defensive*)   What wasn't?

Jack   Don't. You were innocent. It was him. Your fucker of a father.

Jill   We mustn't speak ill of the dead.

Jack That's what they're there for, my love. They're the only ones it can't harm. We have to do it for our own sake. Go on, nail the bastard. Nail him down. Strike a stake through his heart. Have done with him once and for all.

Jill You want me to judge him?

Jack I want you to stop judging yourself.

Jill *shakes her head but it's more like someone breaking out of a dream.*

Jill How?

She shudders and begins to sob. He holds her.

Shirley (*finishing the vol-au-vent*) What about you, Jimmy? What you going to do, luv? Will you go looking for Wally?

Jimmy Is that a joke?

Shirley I don't know.

Jimmy I don't know. It's all a bit much. It's like I'm trying to catch up with meself, but by Christ I'm running fast away.

Shirley What gets you going, Jimmy? It in't me. It won't ever me, not really.

Jimmy What were it then? (*Pause.*) I dunno. Got a kick of sorts out of mekin' them pictures.

Shirley Then go for it. Never know, might even make a bob or two. Tony, coun't Jimmy get his films on the Internet like your fella?

Tony Not impossible. With tonight's exposure, it could be a hot site.

Jimmy Yeh, but I'd want to make 'em proper, fed up with the cheapskate, and I an't got the gear.

Tony You have for now, my friend. And it comes with an experienced porno cameraman.

Emma What are you doing, Tony?

Tony   I've got to earn a livin', petal. And it's a sight more honest than my last job.

Jimmy   I woun't just be in this for the money. I'd like to feel I've got summat to offer.

Edward   Beyond promoting spin-dryers.

Jimmy   You know, Eddie, maybe I can't speak demonic like you, but it don't mean I don't have things to say.

Edward   No. You're right. I'm a patronising little shit.

Jeni (*astonished*)   Will wonders never cease?

Edward   Listen, maybe I could help you, I don't know, clarify what you want to say.

Jimmy   Knowin' me I won't know 'til I've said it. And even then . . .

Edward   That's perfectly legitimate. Leave articulation and justification to us critics. You simply put up the stark transgressive images that raise the fundamental questions. Eros. Thanatos.

Jimmy   What?

Edward   Yesterday's porn, Jimmy, is often today's masterpiece.

Emma (*quietly*)   Yesterday's masterpiece is often today's porn.

Edward   Exactly. That's the debate. Take Titian for example.

Jimmy   Did he make hard core?

Edward   Cunningly disguised as religious epics.

Jimmy   Ah, well now, religious epics, yeh, got to be. God, I'll gi' that John Mills a run for his biblical orgies.

Jeni   I knew we'd end up with sandals.

Jimmy   Got a great location here. An oasis in the holy land. What you reckon, old girl? Can I tempt you into a farewell performance, my lovely?

Shirley   Jimmy. I'm out the business, pigeon. I'm walking the streets. You know what I mean. How can I make it clear? I just want to be alone.

Jeni   Greta Garbo.

Shirley   No. Shirley Thornton née Dunstan.

Jimmy   Fair enough. More than fair.

A beat, then **Jimmy** *turns to look at* **Jeni**.

Jeni   Well, bless you for the thought. But I've already done one sex film, and I don't want to be typecast.

Edward   And don't look at me.

Jimmy   I won't!

Tony   What about a part for the Scarlet Woman? The Great Whore of Balham?

Emma   How long are you going to hate me?

Jack (*suddenly*)   Hate is only love angry.

Silence as everyone turns to look at **Jack** *and* **Jill** *in front of the stained-glass doors.*

Jack   Sorry. Came out sounding a bit like the title of a sermon, didn't it? (*A beat.*) It is actually. Sorry.

Jill *takes his hand. He turns to her.*

Jimmy   Bugger me, it's staring us in the face. Adam and Eve. The love story!

Edward   Strictly speaking, Adam and Eve is hardly a love story, is it?

Jill   Forgive me.

Jack   Sorry, can't do that.

Edward   Forgive me, vicar, but am I not correct in saying that once they eat of the forbidden fruit of knowledge, which we interpret to mean the loss of innocence into experience, carnality, God expelled them from Paradise.

Jack   Not only Paradise but life itself. He created death as a punishment.

Jill   You have to.

Edward   Eros. Thanatos. Powerful themes. But is it a love story?

From now on no one pays attention to the upstage couple.

Jack   Nothing to forgive.

Jill   I corrupted you.

Jack   I'm still as white as the driven snow.

Jimmy   Hang on. All depends on the POV. Point of view.

Jack   I'm a bit amazed about that myself, but there it is. Sorry to disappoint you. Can't seem to do anything about it. (*Smiles.*)

Jimmy   Now at present, the whole story's all shot from the 'omniscient', the God POV, how he sees what the young-uns are up to and how he judges them. And once he's caught them in delicatessen, which he could hardly be fucking surprised about seeing he's put two steamy kids wi' no knickers on running around his garden, then he chucks the buggers out and tells them to sod off and die. Now from where I'm standing I'd say God's POV is a teeny weeny bit over the fucking top, woun't you?

Edward   You wouldn't have said that half an hour ago.

Jimmy   Good point, not saying we all can't go a bit funny when you feel you've been fucked over. Undeniable is that, in't it, Tone?

Jill   Is that true?

Jeni   So God was just jealous, was he?

Edward   And possessive.

Jack   And it's the same with you.

Jimmy   Maybe he was just pissed off he missed the action. Whatever, fact is I'm not going to tell the story from his point of view. We shift it.

Jeni   To what?

Jimmy   To the kids'. It's not about just fucking with them, right, it's about true love. Adam and Eve. Listen to the names. Made for each other. You can't say one without the other.

Jill (*softly*)   Adam?

Jack   Eve.

She reaches out to him.

Shirley   But for them it's a tragedy. Exiled to death for their love.

Jimmy   No, no, Shirl, you know me, I don't want to do nought miserable. Any film I make the spin-dryer has to work at the end. Gi' us all some hope.

Jeni   Paradise Regained.

Jimmy   What?

Jeni   They find their way back to the garden.

Jill   What are we going to do?

Jack   I'm not leaving them. Even if they kick me out I'm not leaving.

Jill   You're a good man.

Edward   Perhaps even the return of innocence.

Jack   We're going back.

Jeni   The return to innocence?

Jill   Welwyn Garden City.

Jeni   Yes.

The iced windows and walls slowly vanish as though a hot dawn is rising. Behind the disappearing doors is now an apple tree that suddenly has burst into both blossom and fruit. **ADAM** *and* **EVE** *are returning to the garden, while the rest dream on its possibility.*

Edward   Brilliant. Now at long last we're getting political. There's your film, Jimmy, *Adam and Eve Part Two: The Return to the Homeland.*

Jill (*murmurs*)   Welwyn. Welwyn . . .

Emma   How do they get in? (*As* **Tony** *turns to watch her.*) I just wondered . . . What happens? Does God just hand them the keys?

Tony   And throws in his Bentley for the journey.

Emma   I'm trying, Tony.

Tony *nods.* **Edward** *is playing with various lighting effects, following* **Jimmy** *around.*

Edward   Trying to create some atmosphere.

Jimmy   No, no, sod the keys, hate the keys business, always have, no, we need a really dramatic start. What about – Tone, can we do this? – tracking shot across the snow outside our indoor Paradise here to the iced-up winders, then hot breath on the ice and first we see of them is their little pouting mouths pop pop pop breathing, melting, two frozen faces, poor little fuckers banished to the blizzard, so cold even his *cajones* are cracking – I'm touching on me own personal life experience here – and, my God, are they fucking desperate, life or death, straight choice, see it in their eyes, then cut to shot from their POV through the circles of melted ice into the warmth and luxury of the indoor garden, then close-up as they suddenly smash their way through the window and mid-shot from within as they climb through back into their garden. Uncertain, the lovers enter Paradise.

Edward   I'm not entirely sure we can actually break windows. The place isn't ours. It's National Trust.

Jeni   We're members of the National Trust.

Edward   Fine line.

Jimmy   Cross it. They just walk through like the window doesn't exist any more.

Tony   One hell of an SFX.

Jeni   What's that?

Tony   Special effect.

Jimmy   But it can be done?

Tony   Nothing's impossible.

Jimmy   So now they're inside. And it's the first time we get a clear shot of them. Master from round here somewhere. First, stock still. Like two frozen alabaster statues. Classical, like. For a minute can't tell them from the real thing.

Jill   Where are we now, Jack?

Jack   Oh, I can answer that, that's dead easy. I love you. And you love me. You didn't know that, did you? (*Smiles.*) But now you do.

A beat, then a gentle embrace. The two slide down out of view.

Emma   And what are they wearing?

Jimmy   Fuck-all.

Shirley   Not even fig leaves, then?

Edward   No. He's right. Clothes would set too many other questions going. This lets the audience relate directly to the mythic dimension.

Jimmy   So they're in. They're melting like they're coming alive. And strangely at same time the whole fucking world around them is melting and coming alive. The ice on the windows turns to a spring shower. The trees outside are revealed in a warm dawn light, the knackered apple tree suddenly bursts into both blossom and fruit at the same time and the lovers are twisted and entwined like snakes about each other.

Shirley   That's beautiful, Jimmy.

*As **Jack** and **Jill**'s clothes appear over the potted plants.*

Jeni   Another SFX?

Emma   Post-production job. No worries.

Tony *turns to look at her.*

Edward   I see where you're going, James. You start with what seems to be a traditional patriarchal allegorical form and then slowly subvert it into a new kind of poetic realism that challenges the very myth of theocratic creation – that the tree is transformed not by supreme power but by the essential yearning of all humanity. It's a metaphor of poetic romantic transcendence refuting all postmodernist ironies.

Jimmy (*unsure*)   Yeh, right, spot on, pal. And we can still end on the fuck, can't we?

Edward   Oh, yes.

Jill (*voice*)   Yes. Yes. Adam. Yes.

Jimmy   Oh, good. For a minute there . . .

Jack (*voice*)   Eve. Eve.

Emma   Will you get her to wave to us?

Jimmy   Yes, of course! Thank you. She's all right, your missis. Yes, has to be. Now they've reoccupied Paradise it has to be for all of us, dun't it? It may just be the two of them but they're fucking like rabbits for us as well. Mam and dad of the lot of us. Bless them. And that's it, got to be

the final shot. Last shot as she rises up on top of him all
dappled and she smiles at us and gi's us a wave. And then
she comes and we have the big scream, waves crashing
down her spine, head spinning like the bloody *Exorcist*, all
that stuff, and we crack up the title song, swelling orchestra,
'Back to the Garden'. Sudden blackout. Classic.

Jill *rises up, silhouetted by the rising dawn behind her. She waves. She
holds the position.*

Shirley   Does it have to end on a climax?

Jimmy   What? Come on, Shirl, you know you always
have to have the big finish. That's what the audience come
for. Orgasmic. That's why it's called climax. They'll all be
expecting it.

Shirley   That's the problem. Sometimes getting what you
expect is a bit disappointing.

Emma   And it's a very traditional male ending.

Jimmy   What other ending could you have?

Emma (*pauses, then*)   A feminine ending.

Jimmy   What's that?

Emma   It's when a piece of music doesn't end on a major
conclusive strong chord, but goes for a minor key that leaves
things more incomplete, open.

Edward   Uncertain?

Emma   Yes.

Jimmy   Why would anybody want to end ought like that?

Jeni   It has its own kind of beauty.

Jimmy   I'm not sure. I don't know.

Shirley   Risk it, Jimmy.

Jimmy   What if it doesn't work out? They'll be wanting
their money back for coitus interruptus?

Shirley   That's life, Jimmy.

Jimmy   Well . . . (*Sighs.*) Not convinced. But . . .

Jill *disappears.*

The lights slowly fade around them as **Edward** *plays with the controls.* **Shirley** *sits down by* **Jeni** *and* **Emma**. **Jeni** *puts her arm around* **Emma**, *and* **Emma**'s *head falls on to her shoulder.* **Tony** *watches* **Emma** *from the other side of the room.* **Jimmy** *looks straight out at the audience.* **Shirley** *sings unaccompanied, smoky, chanteuse-style. Very slowly,* ADAM/**Jack** *and* EVE/**Jill** *will rise up, and become the living embodiment of the original stained-glass doors.*

Shirley
   We are stardust
   We are golden
   And we've got to get ourselves
   Back to the garden.

As **Shirley** *sings with* **Jeni** *occasionally joining in.*

Jimmy   So we're still using the song, are we?

Jeni   Yes.

Edward (*eventually*)   With or without the postmodern irony?

Jeni (*as they all listen*)   I'm not certain.

All are still. ADAM *and* EVE. *The others gazing out. The sun rises in all its splendour, turning all to a frozen tableau of separate silhouettes except for the lovers holding hands.*

Blackout.